The Laundromat Bible

The Laundromat Bible

HOW TO FIND, BUY, AND RUN A SUCCESSFUL LAUNDROMAT

MARK CSORDOS

ISBN13-9798882871955

Foreword

Mark Csordos is like every member of the Coin Laundry Association I've met in my 32 years on the staff here at CLA coaching first-time launderers – utterly unique and bringing his own singular experiences to the laundromat business. Taking what one's learned through life's travails and triumphs and then applying those lessons to our endeavor, where the primary goal is to deliver customers time-savings and convenience in a clean, safe environment that's close to home, is the aspect of the industry I love most. Doctors, lawyers, plumbers, teachers, marketing executives – and yes, even secret shoppers – have made productive, profitable careers in the laundromat business fueled by their own distinctive journeys.

The laundromat business is simple - but it's not easy. The keys to success are evident. In short, choose a location convenient to your client base; keep the facility meticulously clean; ensure that all the equipment works all the time – and treat customers with the dignity and respect they deserve. Executing that vision is what separates the most successful and profitable operators from the also-rans. Done the right way, owning a laundromat (or two or three!) can deliver a rewarding entrepreneurial experience and the profitability that supports a more flexible lifestyle that so many crave today.

This clear, comprehensive volume can guide you through the critical early stages of your journey toward laundromat ownership. *The Laundromat Bible* takes the aspiring laundromat professional through the basics in a manner that is both practical and peppered with real-life experiences – and a welcome dose of humor requisite to surviving small business ownership. Combined with a willingness to confess mistakes honestly, this makes for a great place to start your own trek toward turning dirty clothes into dollars.

Brian Wallace, President/CEO at Coin Laundry Association

Table of Contents

The "Let's Get It Out of the Way" Page

If you're like me, you love to read and learn. I don't like reading a book that is just an advertisement for the author's services, whatever they may be. So, I promise this will be the only time I mention what I do in the book.

I am available for coaching if you want to work one-on-one with me as you move through your laundromat journey. I would also be happy to speak to your organization about topics other than laundromats, such as guerilla marketing and customer service.

Please feel free to connect with me on LinkedIn. Just let me know that you found me through this book.

You can also email me at MarkCsordos@gmail.com.

My website is www.MarkCsordos.com. There are several helpful checklists on the website that you can download. I discuss them in this book, and they're available on the site, so you can easily print them out.

Please subscribe to me on YouTube: www.youtube.com/@markcsordos or Laundromat Entrepreneur.

And, if you are ever in Central New Jersey, come swing by my store at: 1055 Route 34, Aberdeen, NJ 07747.

Now that that's out of the way, let's talk laundry.

About Me

After graduating from Rutgers University, I started my first business, C&S Mystery Shoppers, Inc. First, let me tell you what mystery shopping is because we'll discuss it later in the book.

Mystery shoppers evaluate a business's customer service based on preset criteria. For example, our first client was Pizza Hut. We were hired by the owner, who had multiple locations. We would go into one of his Pizza Huts, as any other customer would, except we were looking for things such as how quickly we got seated and how long it took to get our food. Did the waitress suggest add-ons such as the salad bar or breadsticks? Were the bathrooms clean? This would go into a report with comments and a score to be sent back to the owner. He now had an objective picture of a customer's experience in his restaurant. If he had walked in himself, he wouldn't have been treated like a regular customer because all the employees knew him. Nobody knew who the "secret shoppers" were or when we would visit.

This particular franchisee owned eighteen Pizza Huts, which we shopped once every four weeks. Based on our reports, he could not only tell which restaurants were doing better than others, but he could also zero in on any company-wide issues. Let's say in 50 percent of the visits, the waiter didn't suggest extras like the salad bar and breadsticks. He knew this had to be addressed company-wide since they were leaving money on the table by not upselling.

We also worked with ShopRite (a large Northeastern grocery chain), Manhattan Bagel (at the time publicly traded), the New Jersey State Lottery, and the New York Waterway, as well as many mom-and-pop restaurants and stores. Hopefully, at this point, you aren't putting the book down to start a mystery shopping business because I know many people find the idea of getting paid to eat pizza very interesting.

I had success with the business, and we were twice featured in *The New York Times*, *Vogue* magazine (yeah, that surprised me, too), *Entrepreneur,* and about fifty other publications. I sold the business when my wife became pregnant with our first child. Afterward, I authored *Business Lessons for Entrepreneurs: 35 Things I Learned Before the Age of Thirty*, published by Thomson Learning.

I was off to a good start, but little did I know that when I entered my thirties, I'd spend the next two decades in a career wilderness. I tried to start a speaking career, but this was around the time of 9/11, and with so much uncertainty, companies cut their budgets for extras like speakers and trainers. Since I was unknown, I never gained any traction. My wife and I had two more kids, and I had a series of failed business ideas that didn't get too far off the ground. I also had many lower-management jobs that I felt were dead ends. I was correct in that assumption since two of those companies would later go bankrupt.

Things didn't go well on the health and financial front, either. Financially, with struggling business ideas and three kids, I lost my job during the 2008 recession, and our money problems forced us to file for bankruptcy. On the health front, I was diagnosed with severe depression and would be treated for it off and on during my thirties and forties.

In my late forties, I took what I hoped was my last job working for someone else. The pay was decent, and there was a chance for upward mobility. I thought, "Well, this is it. I can put all those ideas of owning a business and entrepreneurship in the past." I thought this might be the job that would carry me to the end of my working days. The problem was that the company was struggling, and I grew increasingly frustrated as I felt I was being wasted there. I wanted to do more, but they wouldn't let me.

Then, I had a relapse of severe depression and was hospitalized.

I went on disability for two months, and during that time, I asked myself why I spent so much energy on a company that didn't value me. Why didn't I take that energy and put it toward my own project? Years before, my wife and I had discussed buying some laundromats, but we weren't in the position to act on it. Now, we were, and I used the time away from work to dive head-first into the laundromat industry. A few months after returning to my job, I bought my first laundromat.

I left that job to make the leap into the laundry industry, and I couldn't be happier. I share this with you because I want you to know that if you choose to go down this road, the future is yours for the taking. There will be a learning curve, but there will also be plenty of people along the way who are willing to help you.

Fun Laundromat Facts

The term comes from the first laundromat in the United States, which was known as a washateria and was opened on April 18, 1934, in Fort Worth, Texas, by C.A. Tannahill.

There are currently about 35,000 laundromats nationwide. Laundromats generate about $5 billion in combined gross annual revenue nationwide.

The term "laundromat" is a portmanteau of the words "laundry" and "automat," which refers to the self-service, coin-operated nature of the business.

The average family in the United States does eight to ten loads of laundry a week.

National Laundry Day is April 15th.

The Coin Laundry Association is headquartered in Oakbrook Terrace, Illinois.

The world's largest laundromat is located in Berwyn, Illinois. It's a 13,500 square-foot space that boasts 140 washers and 170 dryers.

There is a 2019 movie named *The Laundromat*, starring Meryl Streep, Gary Oldman, and Antonio Banderas. Despite its title, it has nothing to do with a laundromat, but I enjoyed it anyway.

The song "Laundromat" was sung by Nivea and produced by R. Kelly. In 2002, it reached #58 on the *Billboard* Hot 100 list. The lyrics use the laundromat as a metaphor for the washing away of an old relationship.

In a *Friends* episode, Rachel kissed Ross for the first time in a laundromat.

The exterior and interior laundromat scenes in the 2023 Academy Award winner for Best Picture, *Everything Everywhere All at Once*, were shot at the Majers Coin Laundry in San Fernando, California.

So, You Want to Own a Laundromat

"Chase the vision, not the money; the money will end up
following you."
—Tony Hsieh, CEO of Zappos

I must admit I had no idea that so many people were interested in getting into the laundromat business. That's been the biggest surprise to me so far in this journey. When I bought my first location, I kept it very quiet. I told customers I was the new owner, but as far as family and my employer went, no one knew. I invited my brother to our ribbon cutting, but I didn't tell my day job until they decided to close the location I was working at and laid me off. After that, I put it out on LinkedIn and let the world know.

Shortly after that, an old friend contacted me about his interest in owning a laundromat. My brother soon asked if I would talk to a friend who was also interested. I remember talking to a customer before leaving my day job, and I casually mentioned that I owned a laundromat. She got excited and told me she was also considering buying one. I've even had customers ask me how to get into the business. Someone else told me his brother-in-law was thinking about buying one. I've been asked about them numerous times on LinkedIn.

Who would have thought?

Here's my question for them and you: Why? Obviously, I think it's a good business, and it aligns nicely with my life and what I want to achieve in business. But why are *you* interested in it? Not everyone is cut out to be a business owner, and that's fine. Some people excel at working for others and don't want all the responsibility and commitment it takes to own a business themselves.

As long as you're coming into this business for the right reasons and feel confident going forward, let's look at some pros and cons of owning a laundromat. You've probably thought of many pros already, or you wouldn't be reading this book. Please don't gloss over the cons. There aren't many, but they are real.

One thing I'd like to add is that when I mention washing machines or washers by weight (e.g., 30-pound washers or 60-pound washers), that refers to the laundry capacity in the machine, not the machine's weight itself. In my store, we have 20-pound, 30-pound, and 60-pound machines.

Pros

Great return on investment. A laundromat's typical return on investment is roughly 20–30 percent and can be as high as 35 percent. Compare that with another popular industry—restaurants—where, according to CSI Marketing, the typical ROI (return on investment) was 11 percent for 2022.

It's simple to run. It doesn't get much simpler than running an unattended laundry. Even if you offer Wash & Fold and Pickup & Delivery, you don't need to be Steve Jobs to run your store successfully.

It's mostly recession-proof. I don't like it when I hear people say that laundries are entirely recession-proof. While it's true that you need to wash your clothes in good and bad times, a Pickup & Delivery customer could downsize to just Wash & Fold, or worse yet, self-service. So, while it's true that you might feel a little pain in a recession, it won't be anywhere near what some businesses will face.

It's not seasonal. Unless you are located by the Jersey Shore during tourist season or by a college campus, your business won't be affected by the seasons. If you offer Wash & Fold and Pickup & Delivery in certain parts of the country, your revenue might go up or down (because winter clothes weigh more than summer clothes), but you won't lose any customers. In Green Bay, WI, instead of washing shorts and T-shirts, it'll be pants and Packers hoodies.

It doesn't require all your time. When I bought my laundromat, I still worked forty to forty-five hours weekly at my regular job. The gentlemen who sold it to me both had full-time jobs and were rarely at the laundromat. You can still work on your outside interests while owning a laundromat.

You get to know your customers. Unlike many businesses, you can really get to know your customers as people. Many of our customers do their laundry on the same day and time every week, and if they stay and wait for their clothes, they have plenty of time to chat. At our location, customers will often run out to do an errand while waiting for their clothes and ask the attendant if they want anything. You will often learn about their major life events, jobs, kids, etc.

Steady cash flow. Many owners note how consistent their sales are. If it's slow on Monday and Tuesday, the loss will likely be made up by the end of the week. People still need to do their laundry, so if they don't come when they usually do, their clothes remain dirty. They're going to have to come at some point. And, if you aren't a large operation with bigger commercial accounts, you have virtually no receivables. Everyone pays when they use the machines or pick up their Wash & Fold.

Low amounts of inventory. Most laundromats have no inventory to speak of. We have branded laundry bags for sale, some detergents for customers to buy, and supplies for our snack and soda machine.

High survival rate. I've seen the survival rate of laundromats quoted as high as 95 percent. Even if that's overstated, the average laundromat has an ROI of 20–30 percent. Even a below-average laundromat could have an ROI of 10 percent, which is as good as an average restaurant.

Your customers do the labor. There aren't many businesses where customers provide the labor and their own supplies, but that's precisely what they do when using your machines.

Cons

It's still a business. While laundromats aren't that complex, they are still businesses, and if you don't treat them as such, they can fail like any other venture. When you have employees, there are certain labor laws you must follow. You must be aware of your competition. You must keep your business appearance up. You have to deal with customers and manage employees.

Working with the public. While you can create a bond with many of your customers, anyone who has worked with the public knows people can be tough to deal with. Not every customer will be your favorite. You will have customers who put in too much soap even though you have signs stating how much to use. People will shove six quarters at once in the slot and then say the machine isn't working. Someone will say their clothes didn't get clean enough even though the last 100 customers to use that machine were fine.

Irregular hours. If you're used to Monday through Friday, 9 AM to 5 PM, you'll have to get used to some new hours. Laundromats often open as early as 5 or 6 AM for people to do laundry before work or school, and close at 10 PM for people doing laundry after work. You're also open every weekend and most holidays. Of course, you can set your own hours, but the fewer hours you're open, the fewer customers can use your service.

Maintenance and repairs. I had a repair person tell me the only way not to break the machines is not to use them. Since that's not very practical, it helps to be handy. If you've ever had something break while still under warranty, you know that even new machines can malfunction. Customers likely won't take the same care in using them as you would, and as your equipment ages, things naturally break more often. One of the worst things a customer can see is a bunch of "out of order" signs all over your store.

It can be expensive. Laundromats are an in-demand business for a reason, and owners of established locations aren't just going to give them away. Depending on many variables, a laundromat with $100,000 a year in profits could sell for between $300,000 and $500,000. Building a new laundromat from scratch can easily cost a million dollars. The equipment is also expensive. In 2023, I was quoted $5,750 for a 30-pound washer, considered a small machine, which didn't include installation. A 60- or 80-pound machine will easily cost over $10,000 each.

Water and energy costs. For some things, you can shop around for a better price. But for utilities, you're at the mercy of the water, gas, and electric companies. In some parts of the country, you might need to consider that.

It's not hard, but it's not *that* easy. Beware of listings for laundromats for sale that mention a completely absentee owner. I remember one that said the owner worked two hours a week collecting money and made $100,000 a year. Who in the world would sell that business? As mentioned in the "Pros" section, you can have a full-time job and own a laundromat. Don't get suckered into thinking you'll collect a few quarters every Friday, and that's all you'll ever do. Machines break. Emergencies happen. Employees call out sick. Someone has to pay the bills and do the bookkeeping.

The laundromat industry is going through a renaissance as more sophisticated business owners are getting into it because of the rapid technological growth. Technology that didn't exist before COVID is becoming more commonplace, allowing people to scale up from one store that took mostly quarters to several locations with integrated software. The best years are still ahead for the industry.

Where Do I Find a Laundromat for Sale?

Great, you're still with me. So, once you've decided to buy a laundromat, the next logical question is, "How do I find one for sale?" I think there are two ways: the front door and the back door.

We'll start with the front door, which is how I started. Many business brokers list businesses for sale on websites such as BizBuySell.com, BizQuest.com, and BusinessBroker.net. I've used all three, and I like BizBuySell.com the most. It's easy to use and has both a free and paid option. When I started looking to buy, I used the paid option, which gives you more information. Also, the Coin Laundry Association has collaborated with them in the past.

My problem with this approach is not the website itself but the listings and brokers you might encounter. This part might get me some angry emails from brokers, but this book is for you, not them. You must take everything you read in these listings with a *huge* grain of salt. Most brokers are generalists. Want to sell a bagel store? They'll list it. Liquor store? You got it. Laundromat, car wash, consignment store? Yes, yes, and yes. The problem is that they aren't experts in these businesses and don't know what to ask when they agree to sell a laundromat. They use generic formulas for "small business" valuations and often just ask the seller how much they want for it.

Another problem is they get 99 percent of the information from the seller. They haven't researched the competition, the demographics around the store, how much the equipment is actually worth, etc. They know very little about the business they are trying to sell. I've even seen real estate agents try to sell laundromats, figuring it would be an easy commission.

Here are a few softball questions you can ask the broker to find out if they know what they're talking about or if they just took the listing: *How did they arrive at the selling price for the laundromat? Have they sold other laundromats? What can they tell you about the store besides what is on the information sheet they sent you?* If they give you a lot of generalities—like "it has a lot of potential and it's in a nice area"—you probably know more about laundromats than they do. You often wind up having to educate the broker during the process. I'm not the only one I know who has encountered this, and I'll give you two examples.

I came across a business that I thought was perfect for my family. It was an indoor baseball facility. It was a great fit since four of the five of us in my family are big baseball fans, and my brother and two nephews could also be part of it. The seller was asking $350,000, and I was interested based on the numbers in the listing. I asked the broker for a breakdown of their numbers and discovered they were "blended." The broker considered COVID and gave me more of an "average" of what the business had made rather than what the actual company was currently making. When I drilled deeper into the numbers (this is without even looking at bank statements or tax returns), I estimated that the business was worth maybe $100,000, tops. When I told the broker, he said he had talked the seller down from initially asking $750,000. Long story short, this business closed two years later without ever being sold.

There are two takeaways from this example. First, sellers often have wildly unrealistic ideas about what their business is worth and pick an asking price out of thin air. Second, brokers don't challenge the sellers too much because they are afraid to lose the listing. In this case, the broker talked the seller down from $750k to $350k, but based on the broker's background in accounting, he had to know that it wasn't worth anywhere near even this lower asking price. I think sometimes they hope to stumble across someone who has some cash but isn't going to do their due diligence and will just overpay. Fortunately, reader, that will not be you.

Another problem with these listings is that they give you very little information. I remember coming across one for a laundromat, and it stated that the location was in New Jersey. For those of you who think New Jersey is small, it's still three hours from top to bottom, leaving a lot of potential area where this laundromat could be.

When you do find a listing that gives you information, it rarely adds up. This is why knowing your numbers is so important. For this chapter, I went on BizBuySell.com and found a random laundromat listing that gave me some information to work with for this example. Unfortunately, it leaves me with more questions than answers.

The seller is asking $275,000 with $125,000 in revenue. The listing states that the new owner can expect a yearly net income of $50,000 based on having an onsite owner-operator before any debt service. In a case like this, you are buying a full-time job because to make that $50K, you'd have to work there. They pay $3,700 a month in rent. Forty percent of the revenue comes from Wash & Fold, and the rest from self-service machines. It also has two employees. So, let's dig into these numbers.

Rent is $44,400 a year. Take that away from the revenue of $125,000, and that leaves $80,600. This rent is too high a percentage of store sales. Ideally, you would like your rent to be no more than 25 percent of the store's sales. In this example, the $44,400 in rent represents 35 percent of sales.

I estimate that water, gas, and electricity are 20 percent of sales. That's a fair amount. That's $25,000 for utilities, which leaves $55,600.

The owner wouldn't be able to get a lease without proof of insurance, so let's say that's $1,500 for the year. That leaves $54,100.

The listing states the owner is expected to clear $50,000 *if they work onsite*, leaving $4,100. This is where I need clarification.

Out of that $4,100, have they paid *every* other expense?

The listing said there were two employees. One, I assume, is the current owner. With what's left, the second employee couldn't work more than six hours a week, even at minimum wage. They also do $50,000 a year in Wash & Fold, which is great, but what about the cost of the detergents and bags for all that? I assume they have internet and phone, so where's that cost? Do they have any repairs during the year? The listing does note that the equipment is between two and six years old, so maybe they've gotten lucky.

They would also have credit card processing fees, since I doubt all $50,000 in Wash & Fold was paid in cash. How about payroll processing fees? They have an employee, and most businesses use a payroll service like ADP. Office supplies? Accounting fees?

With elementary math, I can tell you this business isn't making $50,000 a year in profit. The broker will always put the most positive spin on the listing, but it's your job to ask questions when the numbers don't make sense.

The listing also tells you two more things about this business. First, they do virtually no marketing or advertising, and it's 50/50 whether or not they even have a basic website. There's no money for it. The second thing is that they do everything by hand, and there is no point-of-sale (POS) system. We'll take a deep dive into this later, but the POS system is your cash register and where you store all the sales information. That means when a customer drops off for Wash & Fold, the employee hand-writes them a ticket. Again, there's no money for a POS.

If you buy this location and bring it into 2024, you're going to spend a few thousand dollars for a POS system, which you'll have to factor in. Based on what we just went through, it's hard to see how this business could be worth $275,000. Yes, the equipment would have some value, but not enough to justify the asking price.

This is not to say that every broker is terrible and that every listing is a waste of time. But I gave up on these websites at a certain point because I just couldn't find anything. That's when I decided to give it one more attempt and go through the back door.

Many well-run businesses for sale are never advertised to the public. When you're part of an industry, you get to know other people, and people talk. One laundromat owner might tell another that if they ever consider selling, they should give them a call. Perhaps a distributor knows that laundromat owner A is considering selling and lets owner B know there is a store they might consider buying.

Since I didn't know a single person in the industry, I had to take a slightly different route—one that might work for you. I figured I'd ask the owners if they were interested in selling.

I did a Google search for laundromats within a twenty-minute radius of my house. I didn't want one any further away than that. I simply wrote the addresses down, and other than their Google reviews, I didn't know anything about them, not even the owner's names.

This is the letter I sent. You can see it's nothing fancy:

Hi. My name is Mark Csordos, and I'm looking to purchase a laundromat in Middlesex or Monmouth County. If you are interested in selling or know someone who is, please call me at (732) 555-5555.

Thank you.

Mark Csordos

I put it in a #10 envelope and addressed it "Attn: Owner." I didn't have high hopes for this method, but I figured the only thing I had to lose was twenty dollars in stamps.

I sent out between thirty and forty of these letters. To my amazement, I got five calls back. Four were interested in selling or at least discussing it, and one screamed at me for sending the letter in the first place.

I wound up meeting with three of the owners. One had a coin-only laundromat, and I felt they had way overpaid to get it. I wasn't sure how much due diligence they had done. The sales barely covered the rent, the machines were on the older side, and they had no website or marketing. I couldn't justify their asking price and passed on it.

The second one was within walking distance of my house. I had an enjoyable meeting with the owner. We discussed ballpark numbers, and the price was within my affordability range. He had owned the store for several years and told me he couldn't pull the trigger on selling it just yet. I still text him once in a blue moon, but he's still not ready. This is an excellent example of one that might never go on sale to the public. When he's ready to sell, he already has someone (me) interested.

The third owner was the Goldilocks location—it was just right. I had never been to the laundromat, but I knew exactly where it was because I had shopped in the strip mall for years. Without boring you with the whole backstory, the letter hit them at the right time, and if they got a fair value for it, they'd sell.

The great thing about dealing directly with the owner was that there was no middleman. I didn't have to go through the broker, who would speak to the owner and get back to me, and vice versa. Three months after he called me in response to my letter, I had the keys as the new owner. I also got a better price because the seller didn't have to worry about giving the broker their cut.

I recommend that you try both approaches. You might have more success with the brokers than I did. Even if you don't, it will give you valuable experience in what to look for and what questions to ask.

What to Look For in a Laundromat

So, you have found a laundromat you're interested in. What should you be looking for, and how important is each piece? I'll cover the financials in a separate chapter. There's plenty to unpack in this one. You will find that the answers to some of these questions depend on what you want. You will also review many of these items during your due diligence.

Do You Want an Attended or Unattended Laundromat?

An unattended laundromat is about as easy as it gets. You need to make sure the coin/change and vending machines are stocked and that the machines are in good working order. If you live close enough, you can clean your store daily or hire a service.

An attended laundromat means your employee (or you) will work at least some of the store's open hours. Having an employee comes with more responsibility and adds a layer of complexity. There are laws you have to follow when you have employees. Employees also need to be trained, and what will you do if your attendant calls out sick the morning of their shift?

How Close Should You Live to The Store?

It all depends on how involved you plan on being. I remember driving an hour to look at a store and thinking, *How would I ever do this if I got a call at dinner time that there was a problem that needed my attention?* I like to be involved, so I wanted one within twenty minutes of my house. The more hands-off you plan on being, the farther away the store can be. If you have a POS system, you can monitor what is happening in the store from anywhere.

Location, Location, Location

You want to be in a location that is easily seen from the road and has plenty of parking. You don't want to have a store that's tucked away, and have customers say they didn't even realize there was a laundromat there. How is the surrounding area? Is it safe and well-lit? Would you feel comfortable walking to your car after collecting money from the machines? If you don't feel safe, then your customers won't either.

Is it a lower- or higher-income area? Neither one is necessarily better. A lower-income area will probably use the self-serve machines more. A higher income area might lean toward Wash & Fold or Pickup & Delivery.

One thing people always tend to associate with the need for a laundromat is a lot of nearby apartments. Apartments aren't automatically a bonanza for business. What's more important is the type of laundry facilities the apartment complex has. If they're in a poorly lit basement, cold in the winter, hot in the summer, and one of the machines is always broken, jackpot! In contrast, larger complexes can have separate laundry outbuildings with newer machines, TVs, and bathrooms. You probably won't see those residents at your store.

Is the location you're looking at in a stand-alone building, or is there some kind of anchor store or surrounding businesses that will bring people to your area? Are you in a mall that has a supermarket or a Walmart? These two types of stores bring in more foot traffic than any other retailers. Many people might come to your location simply because they can run and pick up a few items while washing clothes. I'm fortunate with my location—it's within a mile in either direction of two supermarkets, several banks, a gas station, and a Starbucks. Customers can easily knock out several errands while waiting for their laundry.

Demographics

You might hear a lot about demographics in your research on getting into the industry. This was more important in the past, but Wash & Fold and Pickup & Delivery options open stores up to a much more significant customer base (I will cover Wash & Fold and Pickup & Delivery in great detail later). In the past, laundromats were primarily self-serve, and maybe the store did enough Wash & Fold to cover the salary of an attendant. In this case, having more renters around your store than homeowners would make sense. Today, though, there's a lot of money to be made doing people's laundry for them (Wash & Fold).

One thing to consider is population density. If your store is in a less populated area, there might only be so much you can do to increase sales and profits because there are only so many customers to sell to. A densely populated area doesn't have that problem.

Another thing to look at is whether there are a lot of schools in the area. Lots of schools mean lots of families, and they produce lots of laundry. Busy parents don't have time to do laundry, which can mean lots of Wash & Fold business for the laundromat. Areas like this also tend to have more businesses producing laundry, such as restaurants, physical therapists, gyms, etc.

Lower-income areas will tend to have more self-service customers. Middle- to upper-middle-class areas will tend to have more Wash & Fold and Pickup & Delivery customers because they can afford to pay for it in exchange for the time savings.

The biggest thing that would scare me demographically is an area in decline. You might say the area has seen better days—many stores have closed and there are lots of empty buildings. Or, they closed one of the schools because there weren't enough kids. You can work with most demographic situations and guide your store accordingly, but you can't do much with an area in decline.

Competition, or lack of competition, is not necessarily good or bad. I live within walking distance of two laundromats. They are so close that, for fun, I counted how many steps there were between them (it's about 400 steps). You might think they have to fight it out for customers, but both have been in town as long as I can remember. There's enough laundry for both of them to thrive. It's like when there is a Walgreens across from a CVS or gas station on each corner.

Conversely, the lack of a laundromat doesn't automatically mean the neighborhood can support one. I'd do my research and see if the area has previously had a laundromat and what happened to it. You can go to your township and find out if anyone has applied for permits or is looking to build a new laundromat. You don't want to be blindsided by a new store popping up in six months a couple of blocks down the road.

Reputation and Reviews

Once you find a location you are interested in, one of the first things you should do is check their online reviews. Look for trends in the reviews because anyone can get one negative review. If they have 4.7 stars on Google with forty-three reviews, then they probably run a good operation, at least as far as customers are concerned. If they have a low score and bad reviews, you'll want to know why.

Sometimes, the score can be deceiving. If they have a bunch of one- and two-star reviews from seven years ago, that can weigh the average down, especially if there aren't many reviews. You want to look at reviews from the last year. If they're mostly four and five stars, then you can feel confident that the issues from the past have been addressed. If there are a bunch of recent one- and two-star reviews and the comments are "it's always dirty," "the employees are rude," or "the equipment is always broken," then at least you know what you are dealing with. For me, this isn't a deal breaker. If I were to take over, I would just know that there were some things that needed to be fixed. Sometimes, these are easy fixes the current owner just doesn't want to bother with.

The reviews are just a part of the business's reputation. For any laundromat, you'll first want to experience it as a customer. I did this with ours before we bought it—I had my wife go in separately to get her opinion. You don't have to stay long. Just bring some clothes and throw them in the dryer for twenty minutes. That gives you time to roam around and inspect the place. If they have an attendant, chat them up by asking innocent questions like, "Are they keeping you busy?" That could lead to valuable information. Maybe the attendant says it never stops. That's something you'd love to hear. What if they say they haven't been as busy since that new place down the road opened about a year ago? That would be valuable, too.

Should You Buy the Laundromat and the Building?

In most situations, buying the property and the laundromat together makes sense. You have to run the numbers and see if it makes financial sense for you. For many owners, it's nice to be your own landlord. Just realize that most laundromats aren't sold this way. If it's part of a strip mall, you won't be able to buy the whole mall just to avoid paying rent on the laundromat. Normally in these situations, you would value the laundromat as one business and the building/property as its own revenue-generating real estate and then add the two values together. In these cases, getting a real-estate loan is sometimes easier because even if the laundromat doesn't work out, the land still has value.

Do You Want to Buy an Existing Laundromat or Build a New One?

There are advantages to both. You can design a new laundromat any way you want, and I've seen some beautiful, brand-new ones (yes, I have a little laundry envy). Everything will be pristine, and maintenance will be the lowest it will ever be. When you purchase an existing laundromat, you can do some remodeling, but it's not like simply rearranging the seating area in a restaurant. You can't say, "I think those 80-pound washers would look better up front," and just move them.

The bad news is that if you want to build a new one, you'd better bring a big check. Today's going rate to build a laundromat from the ground up is about $300–$400 per square foot, and it could be higher if it's a really expensive part of the country. This amount includes everything you'd need to go from an empty building to customer-ready. The average laundromat is about 2500–3000 square feet, so you would be looking at between $750,000 and $1,200,000 to build it new. And if you've ever done new construction, you know you'll probably have quite a few headaches during the building process.

If you're going to build a brand new location, you need to hire a company that specifically designs laundromats because there's quite a bit that goes into building one that the average person wouldn't realize. That's why a long lease makes a store more valuable. You can't just put a laundromat anywhere because of all the special infrastructure it needs, and the owner needs to know they will be able to eventually recoup their investment.

No offense to anyone who works for the government, but we all know they aren't always terribly efficient in getting permits processed. A new restaurant was set to open next to my laundromat around Thanksgiving one year, and they didn't open until the following March because of permit problems. You can probably expect a new build-out to take eight to sixteen months from the first shovel hitting the ground to the grand opening. You must also be ready to hit the ground running when you open your doors. The general rule of thumb is that it will take twelve to eighteen months just to break even. With that type of investment, you probably need to be doing $50–55K a month in sales. That's a lot of quarters (you'd probably have a card system or take mostly credit cards, but you know what I mean).

The big advantage to buying an established store, even one that isn't well run, is that you will have customers from day one. If you close the deal on Monday, when Tameka drops off her Wash & Fold on Tuesday and Brian uses the 30-pound washers, that's your money. If you've done your due diligence, you should know how much revenue and which expenses you can expect that first month. With a build-out, you're working on projections. In other words, your best guess.

Can You Get a Laundromat for Free?

"There's no such thing as a free lunch."
—Milton Friedman

Technically, yes, but with a big but. The owner whose laundromat does $350,000 in sales and $90,000 in profits is not giving her store to you for free. She will want several hundred thousand dollars for it, and rightfully so.

What you can find occasionally are distressed or abandoned stores. Why would someone sell you their business for $1? Sometimes, it's because they're in debt, and if you are willing to assume that debt and they can just walk away, they will let you have it. That's why I use the word "technically" when describing this scenario. You can make a YouTube video and tell everyone you paid $1 for this business, but if you assumed $75,000 of debt, in my world, you paid $75,001 for the store. This could still be a great deal. Maybe you, as the new owner, will turn the store into a winner. I just don't want you to think that if you have four quarters in your pocket, that's all you'll need. You will still need to come up with money somewhere in the process.

Another scenario is when an owner just abandons the business. I'm currently looking at a situation just like this. I doubt I will have an answer before this book goes to print about how it plays out, but I will share with you what I am looking at.

There is a laundromat a few miles from my home that a husband and wife owned. I never met them and had never been inside the store. I only found out what happened because I had a few new customers come into my location that had previously used that facility. One day, the store just closed with no notice or warning. One day they were open, and the next, the door was locked for good.

As I mentioned, I hadn't been inside the store. So once I heard about what was happening, I drove over and looked through the window. It looked like they closed in the middle of a work day. There was a calculator and a Coke can on the counter. There was a basket on top of a dryer filled with pillows. It was almost like aliens abducted them. I asked a few employees at the nearby stores, and no one knew anything.

I learned from the building owner that he was suing the owners for back rent. I'm hoping the landlord will just give me the business.

Why would he do that? Because he is in the business of collecting rent and managing buildings. He doesn't want to operate a laundromat. If he decides to get rid of the laundromat, it will probably cost him five figures to remove all the plumbing, venting, and fixtures and convert it to a regular store. He would have to get rid of forty or so washers and dryers, and if he did try to sell them, he'd get pennies on the dollar. It's all just a pain in the ass for him. Wouldn't having someone come in, take over the business, and start paying rent be easier? A situation like this is not without risk. We must ask and answer many questions.

The first question is, what the hell happened? Here is where we need to do some detective work. Maybe the landlord can fill in some of the blanks when the lawsuit is over, but until then, we don't have much to go on.

We know a husband and wife ran it. From their online reviews, they ran a nice little shop. We know they weren't paying the rent, but why? Did they gamble it away? Divorce? Illness? Were they nice people but bad at business? Did it suffer from low revenue? The answers to these questions would help us know how to proceed.

Next, what condition is the equipment in? The landlord would have no idea. That unit might not even have electricity or water since those bills aren't being paid. Does anyone have a financial claim on the machines? If they're being financed, the distributor might want to take those machines back.

How much will it cost us to get the customers back? They didn't stop washing their clothes, so will we be able to get them to return? There are several places they could go, including my laundromat. What would it take for them to switch back?

What will it cost us to update the store? If they weren't paying rent, either because they couldn't or wouldn't, it means that they weren't putting money back into the store. Installing a POS system and getting a new website will cost us money. How old are the machines? Will we have to add some new ones or eliminate some antiques? I'm sure it will also need some TLC to spruce things up.

We would also be flying blind as to their business performance history. Did they make $100,000 in sales a year? Or $150,000? Was it ever profitable?

We will need to hire and train new employees. When they were open, they had strange hours for a laundromat, so I would bet that either the husband or wife was there most of the time. On Tuesdays, they'd close at 3 PM and during the summer, at 6 PM. As a customer, you probably wouldn't go there if you had a day job.

There is a lot to determine before we sign our names onto a twenty-year lease. So, as you can see, there is no such thing as "free." We might be walking into a beautiful situation, or it could turn into a nightmare. It's truly a case of *caveat emptor*—let the buyer beware. If you find yourself in this situation, you should definitely have your lawyer look over everything before you sign on the dotted line.

How to Finance Your Laundromat

There are several ways to pay for your laundromat. You can use your own money or borrow from friends and family. You'd better be able to pay them back, or that will make for some awkward Thanksgiving meals. You can also find a partner who can bring in money.

If you don't have enough to write a check for the whole amount, there are several different sources you can go to for a loan. One option is to get a Small Business Administration (SBA) loan. These are specifically for small businesses. One problem I've seen with these is they often take a long time to get approved. If you want the government's help, you have to go at their speed.

Another loan option is through an alternate lender. You've seen these offers, I'm sure. You're qualified to borrow $100,00 with no collateral, etc. I would do my homework with these because many are legitimate, but if they're willing to give you the money quickly and with no collateral, their loans are usually much more expensive than traditional banks in the form of high fees and interest rates. A reason to consider these is that there are fewer hurdles to jump through, but you'll pay more for the quicker and easier access.

A third option is to go through lenders that specialize in funding for laundromats. You'll find them in seconds if you do a quick Google search. The good news is that since they specialize in laundromats, they might be able to prevent you from doing a bad deal if they don't finance you. Before you apply with them, do your homework and have all your numbers in order. Whereas a local bank probably won't know laundromat-industry specifics, these lenders know them in their sleep. Don't forget that an SBA loan, a regular bank, or a laundromat-specific lender will all require you to put a certain percentage of your money into the acquisition. They aren't just going to lend you $200,000 for a $200,000 purchase. More realistically, they'll want you to invest at least 25 percent of your own money. They want to know you have some skin in the game. If you're a first-time business owner or new to the laundromat industry, they might require you to submit a business plan.

You might want to consider a home equity loan if you're a homeowner. Most people will say never use your home to finance a business, but I wanted to put it out there as an option. Obviously, it depends on your situation, your equity, and how much you want to use. The good thing about home equity loans is that you simply have to apply and be accepted, and you can use the money for anything you want. The bad thing—which is why people say to avoid it—is that your house is on the line if your business fails and you can't pay it back. That's why this option won't be for everyone, and it depends on your financial situation.

Not everyone knows this last one, and many sellers won't advertise it, but it's seller financing. Statistics show that 60–90 percent of small businesses sell with this type of financing. Let's say a business wants $500,000, and you only have $250,000. You ask the seller to hold a note for the other $250,000. The note usually lasts for three to seven years and is paid back with interest.

There are two great things about seller financing. One is that you use someone else's money and can repay them through the business's earnings. This allows you to buy a larger business than you could with just the cash you have in the bank and what you can borrow in loans.

Secondly, if the owner is willing to finance part of the deal, they have confidence in the business and you. If they're waiting years to get the rest of their money, that tells you they feel the business will be around going forward because they still have an interest in it.

I understand why a seller wouldn't advertise up front that they're willing to finance the deal. I'd rather have $500,000 today and never look back. But the reality is most businesses aren't sold that way. I'd prefer to get $250,000 today, and monthly payments with interest than get nothing because I wouldn't budge on the deal structure.

You're Going to Need More than the Asking Price to Buy Your Laundromat

Let's say you find your laundromat and agree to a price. You will pay $200,000 with $100,000 down and the other $100,000 payable over three years with interest in owner financing. That's great! But you will still need more money to get started, and I don't think people always think about that part. They see a business for $200,000 and think, "I could probably swing that," but they don't think about the other costs involved.

First, you will want a lawyer who understands small businesses and leases. Don't skimp on the lawyer. One small thing that you didn't foresee could cost you a ton of money down the road. I remember reading both the lease and the contract and thinking, *it's all just legalese blah, blah, blah*. But It's Important blah, blah, blah, so let's say $2,000 for the lawyer.

If you have an accountant, let them look at the numbers. Having a fresh set of eyes, they might catch something you wouldn't even realize you missed. My wife works for an accounting firm and tells me about the mistakes she sees businesses making in their books because they're often brought to her to fix. She also sees things that small business owners sometimes try to get away with that the IRS wouldn't allow if they were ever audited. There's an old joke in accounting where a business person asks their accountant how much money the company made, and the accountant responds, "How much do you want it to make?"

You will want water, gas, and electricity turned on your first day, so you have to set those up. Our gas company wanted a $2,200 security deposit because even though the laundromat had been there for twenty years, as the new owner, I was a new customer to them. The electric company wanted $800, and the water company didn't ask for one for some reason. That's another $3,000. I'll make that money back in month twenty-five if I stay current on our bill, but it's money I had to put out on day one. Don't forget the landlord wants a security deposit, too. We needed two months down, which was roughly $7,000.

You also have to fund the business for day-to-day operations. Even though we are well into the electronic era, most laundromats still take coins. On the night of the closing, when I met with the seller, I gave them cash for all the quarters in the store, which was around $2,000. I also set up a petty cash "bank" with tens, five, and singles for $200 and two cash register drawers with $100 each. That's another $2,400.

Don't forget business insurance. The landlord likely won't lease the space if you aren't insured. Even if they did, you'd still be crazy not to have it. Like the funding, some companies specialize in laundromat insurance. Let's estimate $250 since you can set up monthly installments.

So, along with the $100,000 cash for the seller at closing, you'll need roughly an additional $14,650. The good thing is most of that money is in security deposits, and you will eventually get it back. The bad thing is you won't see that money for years. Of course, the size of your laundromat will factor into it because the higher your rent and anticipated utility usage, the larger the deposits will be.

Besides money for day-to-day expenses, I recommend having between $10,000 and $30,000 in reserve (depending on the size of your laundromat). You never know when something will break or if you need extra cash. We needed a new hot water heater within three months of buying my location. I missed that in due diligence, and I regret not hiring a plumber to do an inspection. I don't think the seller realized it either, but I'm the one who had to pay for it.

There also might be things that you have to fix on day one. The previous owner of my store did a nice job. But I still wanted to change things to put our stamp on the place. It's like when you buy a move-in ready home but still want to paint the living room because you're not crazy about the color.

Valuing the Laundromat

Putting a valuation on any small business is challenging. There are general rules of thumb, but many factors go into setting a price because no two businesses are the same. It's not like putting a price on a house. If there are one hundred homes in a development, ranging between 1,600 and 1,800 square feet with three or four bedrooms, you can compare apples to apples to get an estimated value. One house might have a new kitchen and a pool, which must be factored into the valuation. But if the last five houses in the development sold for between $395,000 and $421,000, your home likely isn't worth $850,000. For a laundromat or any small business, you could have two on the same street, and one could be worth multiple times more.

The tricky thing about valuing a business is that the buyer could come up with one price, the seller another, the broker a third, and a sales consultant a fourth, and none of them would necessarily be wrong. Ultimately, a business is worth what someone is willing to pay.

For this chapter, we will assume that we have the correct numbers. I will focus on a few things that will impact the valuation in more detail in its own chapter on due diligence.

First, the price the owner is asking is a starting point, not necessarily the selling price. Unlike the housing example, where home price listings are mostly grounded in reality, the asking price for a small business is often picked out of thin air. It's ridiculous but true. In the first example in this book, the owner wanted $750K. The broker got him to list it at $350K, so what was that other $400K based on? Nothing. It was just a nice number that the owner wanted. Since he ended the business without selling, it had zero value to a buyer. So again, where did he get $750K?

Laundromats typically sell for 3.5–5.5 times their yearly net income. As you can see, the multiple you choose makes a huge difference. A laundromat with $100,000 a year in profits could go for between $350,000 and $550,000. That's a large gap.

The first thing you're evaluating is the lease. Don't buy the business or sign a lease without a lawyer. Many people can tell you what to look for and what to ask for, but each situation is unique, and your lawyer can save you from making a terrible mistake. If you are negotiating a lease from the beginning, it can be easier to settle on what's in it, but remember, at the end of the day, the landlord needs you as much as you need them. They lose money on unrented space. When negotiating, it doesn't hurt to ask. The worst they can say is, "No." Also, you get zero of what you don't ask for.

The longer the lease, the better. As I've mentioned, there's a lot of special infrastructure required for a laundromat and you can't just get up and move after five years. No one would start a business knowing they could only own it for five years and then have to sell the equipment. You will see many listings for laundromats for sale with two years left on their lease. You can still negotiate to buy the business, but I would be upfront and let the seller know that any deal is 100 percent contingent on you being able to sign a new lease with the landlord. If they say not to worry about it, the landlord will be fine, then you ask the landlord's name and get them involved at the beginning. If you realize the landlord will be difficult or want too much money, it's better to find that out early than waste your time on a deal that won't happen.

An important thing to realize is that just because someone is a landlord doesn't mean they understand the businesses operating in their building. You might have to educate them as to why your laundromat lease isn't the same as a florist. From the landlord's perspective, a tenant who makes a twenty-year commitment to the store and brings in a regular flow of traffic to the business would be ideal.

It also should be priced at fair market value. If you aren't savvy in real estate, I would recommend getting the advice of a local real estate agent. If the seller or broker says the rent is $X, and that it's a great price, how would you know? There's a good chance the seller and broker don't know either. If you have a twenty-year lease at the right price, that's golden (it can be something like ten years, with two five-year options). If you have a twenty-year lease well over market rates, then you have a twenty-year noose around the store's neck.

Your three biggest expenses are the lease, payroll, and utilities. If you're paying too much for rent, you'll struggle to make a profit before you even turn the first machine on. You want a lease that allows you to know how much your rent will be every year. For example, years one and two are $1000 per month, which increases 2 percent a year until the end of the lease. By doing the math, anyone can know what the rent will be in years sixteen, seventeen, eighteen, etc. This gives you the ability to plan out your future. Maybe at some point, you'll want to add new equipment or a service, and you'll know your expenses. Also, if you go to sell the business, the new owner has some cost certainty, too.

Now, take a lease that is for five years with two five-year options, so you are looking at fifteen years total. Let's say this lease is like the other example, and it's $1,000 per month for years one and two, with 2 percent increases annually through year five. If the landlord puts in the lease that the rent for the first five-year option will be based on current market values, you won't know how much your rent will increase in year six. What if it jumps 30 percent for any number of reasons? Could you afford the new rent? Who will you be negotiating with at the time? The landlord you are signing the lease with today might sell the building before the five years are up, and you could be dealing with someone you don't even know. Most experts would say you should have at least ten to twelve years remaining on the lease if you want to purchase an existing laundromat. Leases under a decade contribute little to the value of the laundromat.

Since we are on the topic of leases, there are several more things to be aware of. If it's not in writing, it doesn't count. I don't care how nice the landlord is or how often they've assured you of something. If it isn't written down, you don't have anything. Watch a few episodes of Judge Judy, and you'll learn this.

It's important for your lawyer to explain to you what is and isn't covered in the lease. A commercial lease is not like a residential lease. If you're renting an apartment with a sink leak, you call the landlord, who will send over the superintendent or a plumber. When you have a business and the sink leaks, you call and (pay for) the plumber.

If you choose to sell the business, you want to ensure that the lease allows you to assign it to someone else. The landlord may want to approve this by doing their due diligence on the buyer. They want to ensure this new person can continue paying the rent. That's not unreasonable, and the landlord might not ask for much from the prospective buyer, but if they chose to, they could hold up the process indefinitely. The prospective buyer will eventually withdraw from the agreement if they can't get the lease. You might want to add a clause that the lease assignment will not be unreasonably withheld, with your lawyer defining what "reasonable" is. You can also add a time limit for the landlord to answer, such as ninety days.

Depending on where your store is located you might need a key tenant clause depending on your store's location. Suppose you are in a shopping center with a large grocery store, and that store decides to move, or that location closes. That store drew most of the traffic to that shopping center, and now it's no longer open. You should be able to negotiate that the landlord will terminate your lease or allow you to continue to rent for a lesser amount.

I don't want to get too deep in the weeds about the different types, such as gross or triple-net leases. Your lawyer can explain those. I've mentioned above that the total amount of the check you send to the landlord should ideally be under 25 percent of gross sales. The lower, the better. It doesn't mean if you come across a laundromat that is at 29 percent, you should walk away, but if the number really starts to get out of whack, like mid-thirties or higher, you need to look at why this rent is so high or why the store is doing so little in sales.

Next is the equipment. How old is it, and in what condition? Like everything else we're considering, many variables go into figuring out the value. Usually, the newer the better. Commercial washers and dryers are built to last longer than the ones for your home. The average lifespan is ten to fifteen years, but it's not uncommon for these machines to last twenty years or even more. One variable is whether they are quality brands. In cars, Toyota has a reputation for reliability. Jeep does not. You might be better off with a five-year-old Toyota than a three-year-old Jeep. How much usage do the machines get? A laundromat would like to get a minimum of three turns a day per machine with a target of four or five.

The more usage, the more wear and tear. Have the machines received regular maintenance? Are they fixed by a technician or the owner? The owner doing maintenance is okay if they know what they're doing, but you might find an owner who holds the machines together with spit and glue to save money. Is the laundromat attended or unattended? I see what customers can do to machines when we are in the building. You can imagine what they do when no one is there. Even the part of the country you're in can make a difference. Machines in a humid or corrosive environment might experience more wear and tear than those in a dry or clean environment. Looking at you, Mississippi and Louisiana (they have the highest annual humidity in the country).

Make sure to look at the mix of machines. How many of each size does the laundromat have? The trend in the industry is moving toward larger machines for both washers and dryers. From a store owner's perspective, larger machines have higher vend prices (vend price is how much it costs the customer to use the machine). From a customer perspective, larger machines mean you can wash more clothes more easily and usually for less money. A family of five can throw all their laundry in one 80-pound washer instead of splitting it among three 30-pounders. People tend to gravitate toward the larger machines even when they don't need them.

There is no proper ratio of machine sizes; it largely depends on whom the store serves. If there are a lot of retirees and one-bedroom apartments that you draw from, you're probably okay with a higher ratio of smaller machines. If you draw from families and do a lot of business in Wash & Fold, you'll want more of the bigger machines. What you want to know is if you need to update the mix of sizes. If you think you'll have to pull out five 20-pounders and replace them with three 40-pounders, you must also factor that into the value.

Next, you want to know the owner's benefits or discretionary earnings.

This equals: The pre-tax profit + Owner's salary + Additional owner perks + Interest + Depreciation – (minus) Allocation for capital expenditures

Got all that? So, let's say the laundromat had a preliminary profit of $20,000. The owner might not even get a salary, but for this example, it will be $50,000. The owner spent $5,000 on goodies for himself that aren't business-related. He paid an additional $6,000 in interest to finance equipment or pay back loans on the business. Lastly, he declared $13,000 in depreciation. That comes out to $94,000 in owner's discretionary earnings.

I want you to understand why those things are added back. The profit and owner's salary would go to the new owner. But $5,000 was for Dave Matthews Band concert tickets and courtside seats for the NY Knicks. The new owner won't attend either next year, so we will add that $5,000 back. The old owner had to borrow money to buy the laundromat, and the interest was a business expense, but that doesn't mean the new owner will necessarily have that expense. Depreciation is the amount of value your equipment loses every year until the point where it no longer holds any book value. Depreciation isn't an actual cash transaction, so no money physically leaves the business, but it does help lessen your taxes. You will need an accountant to tell you what is depreciable and for how long.

The last thing we look at is your intangibles or goodwill. Is the store in a nice, safe area with plenty of parking and visibility? Does the store have a good reputation in the community and online? Does the store need renovations? How easy would it be for a competitor to come into town? Some towns might be so restrictive that no one could build a new laundromat. Is there something coming into your area that will draw more customers? For example, maybe the store at the end of the mall that's been empty for five years will be a new supermarket.

How good is the competition in the area? Will you be at any competitive disadvantage that you can see? If the laundromat you're looking at has a new competitor that just opened three months ago with all new equipment, card readers, etc., and you would have to add a considerable investment to compete with them, then I would factor that into the equation as well. If the store's profits were previously $X, then they're probably $X minus some amount since the new store opened; the profits will also likely be less than the previous full year, which you might be basing your multiple on. The owner might be selling because they don't want to invest what is needed to compete. They want to get paid based on what they were producing before the new competition and let you worry about it going forward.

Let's take a theoretical store. Before anyone sends me an angry email, this is just a simple example. As I mentioned previously, five people can have the same numbers and come up with five different valuations. I find the sellers' and brokers' numbers tend to be higher. I wonder why?

The store makes $200,000 in sales and has $50,000 in the owner's discretionary income. The lease is fifteen years old, and the equipment is on the older side, with the average machine being about ten years old. It's in a nice, safe neighborhood with plenty of parking and a good reputation.

It has a good lease at fifteen years; I would give that a five multiple (if it had been closer to twenty, I would have done five and a half). The equipment is on the older side, but it does have many years left, so I give that a multiple of four. The intangibles are good, so I give them a multiple of five. I add the numbers together and get fourteen, which averages out to a multiple of 4.67. The last thing I would consider is the state of the industry. Laundromats still have a bright future, and with Wash & Fold and Pickup & Delivery, there is still a lot of room for growth. Because of this and since laundromats are in demand, I would round my 4.67 to 5. If it were a declining industry or buyers needed help funding, I'd round that number down. In this example, I think a fair value for this laundromat is $250,000 ($50,000 in owner's discretionary income times a multiple of 5).

There are several factors that you shouldn't pay for. The first one is potential. Brokers love to tell you about the store's potential and that if you do A, B, and C, you'll be super successful. My first question is, why doesn't the current owner do this? Potential is irrelevant when it comes to valuation. You are paying for what the *business is, not what it could be*.

The next thing you shouldn't pay for is the broker's commission. They usually get 10 percent, so if they sell the laundromat for $250,000, the broker gets $25,000. The owner can't ask you for $275,000 to help offset the broker's commission. That's between the seller and the broker. If the owner doesn't like it, let them sell the business on their own.

Since it's largely a cash business, hiding money is easy. If an owner tells you that $10,000 a month goes into the bank, but the true sales are more like $11,500, be extremely careful. If they lie to the government, which can fine them into bankruptcy, they will lie to you, too. Only value what you can verify. Many owners try to have it both ways. They try to minimize their taxes, but when it comes time to sell, they have more cash than Apple. Either they pay their taxes and get a higher payout when they sell the business, or they minimize taxes and receive less at sale time on a less profitable business. You can't have your cake and eat it, too.

Also, it doesn't matter what the owner paid. If they paid $300,000 ten years ago, but the business is only worth $200,000 today, that's their problem. You, as the buyer, aren't there to make them whole. They can say they put in $50,000 in new machines five years ago, but to you, they are used machines and aren't worth that anymore.

Zombiemats[1]

A "Zombiemat" is a run-down laundromat that has seen better days and is the type that gives the industry a bad name. They're usually dark, dirty, and poorly maintained. They usually have a high percentage of machines that don't work or don't work well, and if they are attended, it's usually by a stereotypical curmudgeon who isn't all that interested in helping the customer. The online reviews are all awful. These laundromats can be tempting to people looking to enter the industry. The purchase price usually looks low compared to several hundred thousand or a million dollars or more for a well-run, profitable laundry.

The big question is, what happened? Why did the owner let it get in this kind of shape in the first place? Are they putting off reinvesting in the business because a retool will cost too much? Are they just trying to squeeze every last dollar out of the place and then hope someone takes it off their hands? Unfortunately, a small percentage of owners will use the machines until they cough up smoke with their last breaths. If the dryers are way past their lifespan and your clothes aren't dry, tough. Put another quarter in. Are they facing a large rent increase and just want to get out? Have the neighborhood demographics around the store changed, and the business just isn't there anymore?

Besides those questions, there may be other obstacles. If the store is in such bad shape, I'm sure the books are, too. By virtue of being a Zombiemat, you are already behind the competition unless you're "lucky" enough to be surrounded by other run-down laundries.

Then you have to figure out just how bad the condition of the building and equipment is. If you're a novice looking at a store where most of the equipment is two years old, you can be reasonably sure that the

---

[1] Zombiemat is a trademark of Eastern Funding

equipment is in good shape. But with a Zombiemat, the owner may not know how old the equipment is. If you walk around the store and there are a bunch of handwritten notes on the machines that read, "out of order," you could be looking at a major retooling.

If you're a first-time buyer, I would avoid this type of store unless you have professional help. I know it can be tempting when you see a laundromat selling for $60,000 and you think that could be your entry into the industry, but it could be more of a money pit and a nightmare than your dream come true.

Due Diligence

"Trust but verify."
—Russian proverb

According to the Investopedia definition, "Due diligence is an investigation, audit, or review performed to confirm facts or details of a matter under consideration. In the financial world, due diligence requires an examination of financial records before entering into a proposed transaction with another party." This is the most important part of the buying process so *DON'T RUSH IT.*

You've already done some due diligence. You've checked the place out. Maybe you've gone to a competitor. You've looked at some broad numbers the owner or seller has provided. What I'm talking about now is the deep-dive due diligence. You've made a nonbinding offer on the laundromat that the seller has accepted, and maybe you've put down some good-faith money that your lawyer will hold in an escrow account. There is usually a limited time to do your deep dive into the numbers included in the sales contract. You'll have an agreed-upon time to do your research, probably thirty to sixty days. Your lawyer should have written into the offer that you can back out for any reason, and your deposit will be returned.

This part is critical to get right. A mistake here could cost you tens of thousands of dollars or more. This is also your chance to back out if you find something you don't like. Sometimes, the best investments are the ones you don't make. I caution you on this part for two reasons. First, this part sucks. I'm not going to lie to you. No one wants to sit with a stack of invoices and compare them to bank statements and QuickBooks records. For reasons I will go into shortly, you have to. Secondly, sometimes we have to protect ourselves from ourselves. You don't want to be so eager to get the sale over with and open your business that you gloss over this part just to get it done. You don't want to buy out of desperation. If this isn't the right fit for you, you must be willing to walk away.

I hate to have to address this part, but I've seen enough episodes of *American Greed* to know that you should doubt all the numbers you see until they can be verified. Laundromats are still mostly a cash business, and cash can be easily hidden and manipulated. Most people in the business are good people, but you only need to come across that one who isn't to really set you back. There are many parts to look at during your due diligence. I write about some of them, such as location, insurance, and competition in detail in other chapters, but they would also be a part of any due diligence.

What's your gut instinct about the seller and their character? It's a judgment call, but does the seller seem like someone you can trust? Are they open to answering your questions? I would check them out on social media. If they don't have much social media presence, that's not necessarily bad. If they do, are there any red flags? Also, a simple Google search can uncover a trove of information.

Next, why is the owner selling? Are they retiring or moving? Is there an illness or divorce? Maybe they just need time to focus on other business ventures. Any one of these could be valid. As the buyer, you must ensure it's not something they know and aren't telling you. Is that anchor store that brings so much traffic their way finally closing? Is there a new competitor coming into the area, making the owner want to get out while the getting's good? Are the demographics changing and not to your advantage? Does the store need a complete retool, and they hope you are green enough that you won't realize it? This question can go hand in hand with estimating the seller's character. If you're told they are retiring but you find out the owner is only forty-eight, that would raise a red flag to me. People don't usually retire at that age.

The big part (and where you'll need the owner's cooperation) is verifying the financial reports. The owner might share other aspects of the business, such as competition, demographics, etc., with you, but that's no substitute for you doing the research yourself. If the store takes debit/credit cards or uses a preloaded card system (where the customer loads money onto a card and uses it in the machines), that number is much easier to verify.

Since all laundromats take some cash and some only take cash, figuring out the cash part of the revenue is vital. This is when they open their books up to you, and you go through the tedious task of comparing the bills and deposits against the bank statements and tax returns. The most important number on the tax return is revenue. Most people won't inflate that because they don't want to pay more taxes.

Require two years of records. The reason for this is twofold. The first is to verify all the numbers. Second, you can identify year-over-year trends. If in January 2022, the store made $10,000 in sales and the following year it made $10,600, it helps you as the new owner to know what to expect in the subsequent January. If they don't have two years of records, why? Why are they selling it already if they've owned it for fewer than two years? They could have a perfectly legitimate reason, but you need to know why. In this case, they should have the previous owner's records from when they did their due diligence. If they don't, then you have to be extra careful.

One way to look back into estimated sales is through water usage. I debated putting this in the book, but I didn't want you to hear about it elsewhere and wonder why it's excluded here. Using this calculation method is a little more complicated than some people make it out to be, and in the end, it only gives you a ballpark estimate. We'll go into it in detail in the following chapter, but the goal with this calculation is to come within five to ten percent of the actual washer income.

The problem is that if sales are $200,000 and you come up with $180,000, you're within the margin of error, but there's still a $20,000 difference. There are also legitimate reasons these numbers could be off. Hoses and pumps leak. The toilet could run. You could have an old or malfunctioning water heater. But, if you come up with the same $180,000 and the buyer states that sales are $310,000, this would be a big red flag.

Verifying Financials

This chapter takes a closer look at some of the issues you'll want to address during your due diligence period.

Performing a Water Analysis

There are four things you need to perform a water analysis. The first is the total annual water consumption for the store. Second, the percentage of income from each type of washer. Third, the gallons of water per turn for each washer type. Lastly, the vend price for each machine.

The first one is easy to figure out. Simply add up the water usage for the year from the water bills. If your bill is in cubic feet and not gallons, 1 cubic foot of water is 7.481 gallons. If you're in a building that doesn't measure water usage separately, like maybe a shopping center, you can skip this part about water analysis.

Next, you'll need to know the model of every washer in the store and how much water each washer uses per cycle. You're going to have a mix of different size machines, and you might have a mix of different models for the same size machines if they were purchased at different times or from different manufacturers. These washers may also have different load capacities because some can be programmable by the owner, or they may not be set to the manufacturer's default.

Next is the vend price and how many turns a day for each machine. A turn is how many times customers use that machine each day. If the owner has a POS system, the number of turns might be recorded by the system, depending on how it's set up. The owner might also track turns the old-fashioned way, on a spreadsheet. Many owners don't track it all, so you must use the best guesstimate.

In simplest terms, let's say a machine uses thirty gallons of water per cycle, has three turns a day, and the vend price is $4 a wash.

That would be:
356 days/year X 3 turns/day = 1,095 X $4 = $4,380.

So the water usage would be:
3 turns X 30 gallons = 90 gallons X 365 days = 32,850 gallons
If you do that for each machine, you will get an estimate for the total water used and the revenue that was generated from that usage.

There are a few variables that can go into this. One general rule of thumb is to allow about 5 percent water usage for other considerations such as toilets, faucets, leaks, mopping the floors, etc. If vending prices were raised during the year, you'll want to factor that in as well. If every machine went up a quarter on June 1st, then you have to do the above exercise from January 1 to May 31th at the old vend price and June 1st to December 31st at the new price.

If the store does Wash & Fold and/or Pickup & Delivery, you must deduct that from the equation. The good news is that if the owners have a POS system, you can look up how many times each machine was used and how much money each order created. The bad news is that if they handwrite all the tickets, you're back to using your best guesstimate.

This is the formula from the Coin Laundry Association:

BASIC WATER CONSUMPTION ANALYSIS

Here is the simplest method of analysis that uses water consumption to estimate income:

$$\frac{\text{Total gallons of water used per year (minus non-wash usage)}}{\text{Combined total gallons of water used per one cycle for all washers}} \times \frac{\text{Combined total vend price per one cycle for all washers}}{} = \frac{\text{Total estimated annual washer Income}}{}$$

Unscrupulous owners can fudge this number. They can simply let the water run. Run the machines empty and let the water go down the drain. It's a shame to wastewater that way, but some people don't care.

What I would look for is trends. You should have two years' worth of water bills. The laundry industry is pretty consistent, so unless there are special circumstances, you shouldn't see wild fluctuations in revenue and expenses. If the water bill consistently aligns with revenue and then suddenly, water usage goes way up (but sales are roughly the same) three months before the owner listed the business for sale, that would raise a red flag. You should look for a similar pattern, or lack of pattern, with the gas and electric bills. If there is a surge in water usage but the gas bill remains the same, did everyone wash their clothes and leave without drying them?

Count That Money

Another way to verify income is to collect the money with the owner. This system also has its flaws and may not always be realistic. I will admit that, maybe to some people's chagrin, I didn't do this during my due diligence. The idea is that when the owner collects the money from the machines and the register, you count it with them. You can also figure out the number of turns per day by doing this. If the machine has $20 in quarters and the vend price is $4, that means it was used five times. Subtract out Wash & Fold (from the staff using that machine) and divide it by the number of days since the last collection. If it's been two days, then that machine had a daily average of 2.5 turns.

This method's problem is that it's super easy to manipulate. If a seller wants to deceive you, they can simply add quarters to the machines when you aren't there. An even easier way is just to collect the quarters less often. For example, our dryers are stacked two high. The higher ones get used more because you don't have to bend to get your clothes out. If I normally emptied the dryers every Monday morning, I could just skip collecting from the bottom ones so they looked fuller when I did it with the prospective buyer.

The only true way to make sure that the coin boxes aren't "salted" is for you and the owner to open every machine at the start of business ("salted" is a term that refers to the owner adding quarters to the coin boxes before opening them with the prospective buyer present). Then you stay there all day and empty every machine together again after closing. Then, repeat this process several times to get an accurate count.

This is where reality comes in. One of the great things about owning a laundromat is that many owners also have day jobs. If I had asked the seller of my store to do that, he'd have said, "No." Not because he was hiding anything, but because he had to be at his job—he wasn't going to be able to be at the laundromat at 7 AM and then come back at 8 PM to empty all the machines. He also traveled for work, so he could be gone for days at a time.

I was also working, so I wouldn't have been able to do it, either. One thing I could have done was stay on the premises from open to close, write down every machine that was used, and multiply it by the vend price. That would be just as good as actually collecting the coins, but that's a long day, and it might not always be feasible if you have a family, a job, daily obligations, etc. One ancillary benefit of that option is that you'd get a good idea of how the store is run and probably get to talk to some real customers.

Other Income

So far, these methods have counted income from customers coming in and doing their laundry. The store may also offer Wash & Fold and Pickup & Delivery services, which will generate income as well. If the store has a POS system, this income is much easier to verify. Even with pen and paper, they still need some way to track the orders. Don't go just by what you see, e.g., how many bags need to be washed or picked up. If you are new to laundromats, a small amount of laundry for Wash & Fold can seem like a lot compared to what you wash at home, but it might not be that much by laundromat standards.

The first thing I would do is verify every order in the system. There should be a list of laundry that needs to be processed and a list that has already been processed and needs to be picked up by the customer. I'd take the list and look for those orders. Order #4011: Denzel Washington. Check. Order #4012: Nicolas Cage. Check. When we get busy, I sometimes check these myself to ensure we don't miss anything. I wouldn't worry about weighing the bags unless something seems way off. If Jim Jolly's order says it's ninety-eight pounds and it's one bag, I'd check that. It could be just a simple mistake, especially if everything is handwritten.

If the store has Pickup & Delivery, you should either go with the driver or offer to pick it up yourself. If they are big enough to need a driver, then it is less likely they are fudging any numbers. If it's a small route, it's good to verify that these are real customers, and it also gives you experience. I doubt the store will mind if you do their pick-ups for them.

The last thing you can verify is ancillary sales. These are sales you make from behind the counter and through vending machines. Things like drinks, snacks, detergents, laundry bags, massage chairs, video games, or anything else that is not income from people washing their clothes or from Pickup & Delivery and Wash & Fold. This should be easy to verify with receipts. For example, I have an older snack machine that only takes cans. If I bought thirty-six twelve packs of soda and sold each can for $1, I should make about $432 in soda sales minus stock on hand. If you sell laundry bags for $10 apiece and the store ordered fifty during the year and still has ten left, you should have $400 in sales.

If the store has something like a massage chair that you can't verify, ask yourself if the number they give you makes sense. If they tell you it does $20,000 in sales but you've been to the store eight times and never seen anyone use it, I'd question that. If they told you it was $800, that's two dollars a day, so as long as it was working, that would seem reasonable. These things should amount to only a small percentage of store sales. They are mostly there as a convenience to the customer.

Check the Books

At the end of the day, I don't think anything replaces just looking at the books. Hopefully, the owner has a software tracking system like QuickBooks and copies of all their bills. You should request two years' worth of tax records, P&L statements, checkbook registers, and bank and credit card statements. This is where you do the tedious but essential part of matching receipts and invoices to the owner's records. A crucial thing to remember is *you are only going to pay for what you can verify*. If the owner gives you a wink and a nod and tells you "most" of the cash makes it to the bank, don't believe them.

First, that could be an outright lie to make the business look more profitable, and there's no way to prove it. Secondly, if they're telling you the truth, that means they're cheating on their taxes by underreporting income. If they lie to the government—which can heavily fine them (or imprison them in the absolute worst cases)—they will lie to you, too. If their tax return shows $100,000 in income, but they tell you it's really $112,000, too bad for them. They should have paid their taxes because you're using the $100,000 number. Most businesses the size of laundromats are accounting on a cash basis, so what goes into the bank is the revenue number you use.

Another piece of information you can glean from these records is whether everything is being paid on time. If the rent is due on the first, but you see it continually being paid on the 8th of the following month, what does that mean? Does the business have cash flow problems? Is the owner just sloppy when paying the bills?

Don't Forget Expenses

Expenses can be harder to determine because only some business owners are good at keeping the books. Sometimes, they "forget" expenses and sometimes, they don't include expenses that someone else takes care of for them.

For example, let's say someone owned a store in Buffalo but didn't have any expenses for snow removal. It's possible that could be included in their rent payment, but for this example, let's say it isn't. But the store owner has a brother-in-law with a snow plow that will do the lot for her. If watching Bills games in December gives us any indication, they get a lot of snow, so the new owner, who doesn't have a relative that will plow the lot for free, must account for that expense in their calculations.

An owner can also "forget" expenses honestly or because it will help them boost the selling price. When I see a breakdown of expenses, the "big" ones are always included: rent, payroll, and utilities, but there are many little expenses that creep up during the year. The Office of Weights and Measures will inspect your dryers to ensure that the time you are advertising is the amount of time the customer gets. They came to our store. We passed, and they gave us new stickers for the machines and a bill for $400 for the inspection (someone has to pay their salaries).

A store could have their windows cleaned once a month, and they just pay the person out of the register and don't record the receipt, if they even get one. These expenses might not seem like much, but they can add up during the course of a year.

Another thing to consider is how many hours the owner works, and if they're included in the payroll numbers. This could be something that is open for debate between you and the seller. When I look at an attended laundry, I take the number of hours the store is open and multiply it by $15 because in the New Jersey/New York market where I am, that's the minimum wage. A store that's open from 6 AM until 8 PM seven days a week is open ninety-eight hours a week. Multiply that by $15 per hour for fifty-two weeks, and the store payroll is $76,440 (I'll assume, for this example, that there is only one person on duty per shift).

Let's say the owner works six hours a week and doesn't include that in the payroll number. They work on Tuesday and Friday nights by themselves from 5 to 8 PM. They collect the quarters, fill up the vending machines, do some paperwork, etc. They do what an attendant doesn't. They don't do Wash & Fold and will help a customer if they come in to drop off or pick up their clothes. This seems very reasonable to me, but this is where the debate comes in. In this example, the owner works 312 hours during the year, saving $4,680 on payroll (not including the taxes that go with payroll).

This might not be a big deal if you plan on doing something similar. If the owner works thirty unpaid hours a week and you plan to work three just to collect the money and check-in, you must account for those other twenty-seven hours in your expense total. So, a store that claims $100,000 in profits (which is true the way the current owner operates) actually has $83,800 when you account for paying someone for those hours. If we're using a multiple of 5X earnings to value the store, the current owner will want $500,000, and you are actually in the $419,000 range. This is where the negotiations begin.

When it comes to expenses, unless their books are impeccable (and a well-run business's should be), they missed something. This doesn't mean they are necessarily trying to pull a fast one on you, but think about it this way: every dollar of missed expenses will cost you five dollars extra for the business at closing. The lady in Buffalo whose brother-in-law is more than happy to plow the lot for her has been doing it for years, so she doesn't even think about that as an expense. But you'd have to pay $1500 per season for that service, so that would be an extra $7500 on the closing price of the business.

The once-a-month window cleaning paid out of the register probably isn't included, but just $30 a month would mean an extra $1800 at closing. The $400 they paid to Weights and Measures (and forgot to record) would be another $2000. I'm giving you all these examples to show that even the little expenses can add up at the end of the day. If you don't know all the expenses a laundromat can have, I would add a miscellaneous category and assume something wasn't counted.

Cash Under the Table

Let's talk about something else that isn't really discussed, but we all know happens: paying people "under the table" or off the books. Even with the new technology coming into the industry, laundromats are still mostly a cash business. With more consumers today paying for everything by card, the laundry industry has become more visible to the IRS. If you are buying a business that's been paying people under the table, you have to make your first payroll 100 percent above board. If the old owner wanted to take that gamble, it's on them, but you aren't doing it. You also aren't paying for it at the closing. You need to subtract the payroll and taxes that should have been paid from what the owner claims are the profits.

In New Jersey, they're coming down on this. The state randomly inspected us, and they wanted six months of payroll records and employee schedules. They also wanted employee files. Three people showed up on the day they were scheduled to come, and they just sat in the back and verified everything. We didn't have any payroll violations, but we did get fined for other things, so check your state guidelines on what you need if you have employees.

Luckily, much of it is easy stuff you can do yourself. We got a fine because we didn't have a labor poster with all the laws that nobody reads. We ordered one online, and it was an easy fix. We didn't have the NJ sick time policy posted. We printed it out and fixed that. My son was seventeen years and eight months old but didn't have working papers. We never thought about that, but technically, we should have. If you are paying people correctly, that's 95 percent of what they are looking for.

To wrap up the financial part and to reiterate: *you don't pay for what you can't verify.* If they didn't keep good records, that's on them, not you.

Equipment Check

The next thing you want to do is check out the building and equipment. The age of the equipment is just one aspect of evaluating its worth. Are the machines high quality? Has the owner done upkeep on them? Here's where "turns" come up again. A machine that is three years old but averages five turns a day has done the same amount of washes as a five-year-old machine that does three turns a day. To quote one of my favorite movies, *Raiders of the Lost Ark*, when Indy and Marion are finally alone, he tells her, "It ain't the years honey, it's the mileage."

I would hire a third party to check out the equipment. Even if you are handy, which I'm not, you might not know what to look for. Hire someone who fixes these machines for a living and knows their way around a laundromat. I did have someone check out the machines for me, but looking back, I don't think they were that thorough. We walked through the store and he checked things out, but he never even turned on a piece of equipment, and he wound up missing something big.

The hot water heater was literally falling apart, and within three months of the closing, I spent $13,000 to replace it. The back of the water heater was just about to leak through the hull. The previous owner wasn't trying to hide it. I don't think he knew either. He just got lucky that it lasted long enough for him to close the sale, or he would have been the one replacing it. The person I hired should have known enough to look on the other side of the tank. When it was replaced, the gentleman installing it said it was probably the original one and far exceeded its life expectancy. I consider myself lucky that it was only the hot water heater and the rest of the machines were fine, but you can see how one mistake can be a five-figure bill.

You can also request their maintenance records. Don't be surprised if they don't have them, but you should be able to figure out what machines were worked on (and why) by the receipts from the repair company. Regardless of how many turns a machine does daily, the older it gets, the more love it needs. If the owner has all eleven-year-old washers and no repair costs, they are either extremely lucky, which I doubt, or they're doing repairs themselves or hiding the bills. Since this business is selling for a multiple of five, if the owner pays an $800 bill out of pocket, it's worth $4,000 on the purchase price. That's a good return on investment. You might be able to contact the repair company or companies the owners use and ask them for any records they have. They might not be able to tell you what was done, but if they can give you the amount that was spent, you can compare it to what the owner says they spent.

Don't forget the rest of the building when you're doing your equipment walk. This can be easy to do and is logical. If you walk into a laundromat and see several out-of-order signs, it looks bad, so of course, you want all the machines to work.

It's similar to a home inspection, where you get a fifty-page report with pictures. We don't need a report unless they find something wrong, but we want them to check the same things.

Whoever you get—and it could be more than one person—should be looking for various things. In no particular order, we'll start with the roof. A technician should inspect the vents and the soundness of the roof, and check for leaks. There are few worse feelings than having to put buckets down in your store to catch the water leaking through the roof. One quick way to check the roof from inside the store is to look at the ceiling and see if you detect any water stains or mildew. If there is water leaking, it might not be detectable from the top of the roof.

Now, looking down at the floor and basement, you want to see if there are any cracks in the tile near the machines. This could indicate the wrong type of concrete was used for a hard-mount washer. Your laundromat might not have a basement. Mine doesn't, but if you do, you want to look for signs of water or mildew in the basement because this could mean one of the machines has a leak. You also want to ensure the basement has the proper support under the machines. I went into an older store and stood by their large washer (at least a 60-pounder), and I could feel the floor shake when it was in use. My unprofessional opinion then was, "That can't be good."

You will also want to check the electric, gas supply, dryer venting, and plumbing. When it comes to plumbing, laundromats need a two-inch supply line. A plumber knowledgeable about laundromats should check the entire water supply system for leaks, corrosion, and proper sizing and installation. This goes back to why the lease is so important: you can't just "move" a laundromat to a new location like a different kind of store.

Besides all of the systems in the store working, you want to ensure the previous owner didn't fancy themselves some kind of "MacGyver," doing all their own repairs and not worrying about things like permits, building codes, and safety.

You'll also need to ensure that there aren't any liens or lawsuits pending against the store, that the store owns the washers and dryers, and that they aren't leased or financed. If the machines are leased or financed, you'll need to figure that into your expenses if it wasn't figured in already. You will also need to agree with the seller on what bills need to be paid by them, you, or to be split. You will work with your lawyer on these questions.

Keep It Clean

It's important to check wages and employment taxes if the store has employees. Most small businesses work with ADP or another professional service to do their payroll. You don't save much money doing it yourself, and the possibility of errors and penalties is far greater than what you would save. The biggest thing to look for is that employees are being paid on the books and to estimate how many hours the owner works the store. If you know Jane is scheduled thirty hours a week, but the payroll records show fifteen on average, she is probably getting paid under the table. You can't do anything about what happened before you purchased the store, but going forward, you will have to pay her completely on the books, which will cost you extra money.

As far as the owner goes, if the store is open for one hundred hours and payroll only accounts for seventy hours, does that mean the owner is working the other thirty? If they told you they come in to "just collect quarters," it's another red flag.

It's important to realize that unless you have owner financing, you don't have a lot of recourse if something has been misrepresented. Let's say the seller convinced you that they do $10,000 a month in sales, and you find out it's only $8,000. That's probably a big enough gap to keep you from making a profit. Could you sue them? Yes, but realistically, would you? Probably not. You would have to pay a good amount in legal fees, take time from your business, and then prove they lied. The first thing they will likely say is that you don't know how to run the business, and it's buyer's remorse on your part.

In this case, you're better off trying to grow sales to what you thought you were getting in the first place. If you're off by $10,000 a month, you'd probably sue while realizing you did a very poor job of due diligence. This is the reason I love owner financing. They're less likely to play games with the numbers because they want you to be able to pay off their note.

Insurance

No one likes paying for insurance, and I know you'd rather skip it until the day you need it, but there are several types you should have before you open your doors. Like brokers, there are insurance agents who specialize in laundromats, so they will know exactly what you need, but here are a few types you should consider:

General liability insurance for a laundromat provides coverage for third-party bodily injury or property damage claims that may arise on the premises. It typically includes legal expenses and settlements if someone is injured or their property is damaged while at the laundromat. This insurance will also cover damage to rented premises. Liability coverage protects a business if it accidentally damages a rented space. Liability insurance is crucial for protecting the laundromat owner from potential financial losses associated with these damages.

Property insurance for a laundromat covers physical assets like machines, equipment, and the building itself. It's a way for laundromat owners to protect their investment in the physical property and assets of the business.

Business interruption insurance for laundromats provides financial protection when the business is temporarily unable to operate due to a covered event, such as a fire or other significant damage. This coverage helps compensate for lost income and ongoing expenses, like rent or utilities, during the period when the laundromat is forced to close.

Umbrella insurance for a laundromat serves as additional liability coverage beyond the limits of the primary policies, such as general liability or auto insurance.

Workers' compensation insurance for a laundromat covers all employees' medical expenses and lost wages if they suffer a work-related injury or illness. This goes for 1099 employees as well, unless you have proof of workers' compensation coverage through a staffing company. Each state has its own laws on workers' compensation.

If your store has a company-owned vehicle for Pickup & Delivery, you will also need commercial auto insurance, and depending on where your store is located, you might also need flood insurance.

The two most common insurance claims for laundromats are "slip and falls" and fires. Fortunately, there are easy steps you can take to reduce your risks. The most obvious is to clean up spills quickly and always have a mop or towels handy and Wet Floor signs or cones to put around the spill. Often, if these items are accessible, the customer who made the spill will grab them and take care of it themselves.

Equipment maintenance is crucial, especially for the dryers, where most fires start. You must ensure your dryer vents and lint catchers are cleaned regularly.

Another thing that will help protect you is having cameras on the premises. This way, if an accident occurs, you have evidence to document it.

The First Day

"Even the greatest was once a beginner. Don't be afraid to take that first step."
—Muhammad Ali

"You don't have to be great to start, but you have to start to be great."
—Zig Ziglar

The night we closed on our laundromat, my wife and I met the owner at the store. We counted the quarters. He took a few things that were his, handed us the keys, and wished us good luck. When he and the employee left, we just stood around for a bit, taking it in. What was "one day" talk was now a reality. We owned a laundromat. All we had to do next was figure out how a laundromat works.

One big piece of advice I would give any new owner is to spend the first month or two learning about your new business. Find out where things are and how they work. Get to know your customers and employees. You might be full of ideas, but just put them on hold for a bit. You can still implement them later, but you'd be surprised how many little things there are to learn since it's all new. That's why I want to share with you some of the dumb things we did in the beginning—so when you make silly mistakes, you'll know you aren't the only one.

We bought the store in December, so naturally the closing person would shut the water off at night so the pipes wouldn't freeze. One of the first times I opened the store myself, a customer loaded a machine, put her money in, and no water came out. In my head, I was freaking out because I didn't know what to do. Then, a second customer said the same thing. I'm not sure when it dawned on me, but I never turned the water back on. Good job Mark.

Then there was the time I got a text at work that one of the coin machines wasn't working, and my first thought was, "Did I forget to turn it back on when I filled it with quarters?" Because I had already done that once. So when I got to the store, I opened the coin box and it was on, so I was out of ideas. There was a phone number on the machine of someone who had serviced it before, so I called them. I thought, "Please don't make me need a new machine. I can't afford it." When I spoke to the lady, she asked me if I had reset it. I asked how do you do that? She said there was a little red button where the money feeder was; if you press it down, that should work. Crisis averted.

I believe twice I loaded one machine with clothes but put the money and soap in the machine next to it. So, I got to see the drum fill up with bubbles and then spill out like in the movies when I opened the door.

This wasn't me, but an anonymous family member who might read this book was trying to help clean out the lint trays and put the lint key in a coin box instead. The lint key is flimsy, and she must have turned it hard because it broke off into the box. Fortunately, we had extra lint keys, but I couldn't get the broken key out of the coin box. At some point, we would need to be able to get into the coin box because once it was filled, it would no longer allow the dryer to take any more quarters and we couldn't use that dryer anymore.

You'd be surprised how hard it is to break into one of those boxes. We first tried to MacGyver it. We used very thin tweezers and then a paper clip with glue. I called three locksmiths and they all said they couldn't do it (I thought their one job was to open locked things). Next, my wife tried to drill through the lock, and the drill bit broke off inside the lock, too. I'd had a repair company come to service a few machines and asked them to try. They came with a bigger drill and still couldn't get the damn box out. They had to come back to bring a part for one of the dryers, so they brought a device with a circular saw on it this time. Watching the guy get it out was like a scene from a movie. He had on a face shield, and sparks were flying, but he finally got the box out.

I share these stories with you because when you make mistakes in the beginning, realize you're not alone. You have a new store to learn about and a 5-pound bucket of keys that aren't labeled, so take your time and get your footing first.

POS for Your Laundromat

"What gets measured, gets managed."
—Peter Drucker

"It's not that we need new ideas, but we need to stop having old ideas."
—Edwin Land

As you learned earlier, "POS" stands for Point of Sale. It's your cash register and it stores all the information about your transactions. If you already have one, you know how valuable they are. Unfortunately, many laundromats still use paper and pen and the laundromat industry remains woefully behind in the use of technology in 2024.

In high school, I used to work at a supermarket. This was in the late '80s and early '90s. Back then, we would type each individual item into the register instead of scanning it. A carton of milk would be eighty-nine cents, dairy. A bottle of bleach would be sixty-nine cents, taxable grocery. Ground chuck was $1.27, meat dept., and so on. You'd be stunned if you went into Walmart today and the cashier did that. Why would they be using such an antiquated system? Where's their scanner that tells you the price, number in inventory, aisle location, and availability at nearby stores? So why are some laundromats still stuck in the '90s by weighing clothes on an old-style scale where the needle gyrates back and forth until it settles on a weight, and writing all the information on a paper ticket to hand to the customer?

Let's look at this from both sides of the counter. We'll start with the management side first.

There are several good companies out there that have developed POS systems specifically for laundromats. I use one, and I've received demos of two others so that when I coach individuals, I can speak intelligently about their services. You can find them in five seconds with a Google search. What I won't do here is compare and contrast what they each do—because they keep updating the systems as they grow, and depending on your needs, they have different price points. I will discuss what they *all* do and why they're so important to manage your business.

It's 2024, and if you are still writing everything down, you can only guesstimate your business. The Peter Drucker quote at the top is so simple yet so profound. Here's a little example: I was running a report on everything we had sold year to date. It told me how much we did in Pickup & Delivery at each price point. How many dog beds or blankets did we clean, what were the total sales, and so on? I looked up blankets and asked my staff how many blankets they thought we'd processed so far that year. I got numbers ranging from 250 to 6,000. The actual number was 689.

Why is that important? Because that represents over 15 percent of our Wash & Fold business. Blankets are a very valuable part of our business, and maybe I could lean into that more. Another thing I found was that we had done roughly eighty dollars in pet beds. We didn't even wash the one we have for *our own* dogs. Roughly 44 percent of American households have at least one dog. Going forward, it could be a big opportunity for us if we promote that service. I wouldn't have known this if we didn't have a POS keeping track of it.

The second thing having a POS system does is allow you to collect all your Wash & Fold and/or Pickup & Delivery customers' information. This makes it easy to store customer preferences and to send them text or email marketing. Let's say, for example, Jane doesn't want the attendant to use any fabric softener when her clothes are cleaned, and she wants all the collared shirts hung on hangers. This information is always shown when you print out the ticket to put on her bags. If the tag is handwritten, she has to remember to tell the attendant at drop-off, or you will have to ask each time she comes in. Maybe, for some reason, Jane has special pricing. That would also be stored in the system.

I'm at home writing this, but I will toggle back and forth to show how the POS system allows you to manage your business from anywhere. I can log on from any computer or mobile device and see there is still one eighty-four-pound order that needs to be worked on for delivery tomorrow. We have 117 additional pounds of laundry due tomorrow, and I can see that one order is in the washers right now, and one is in the dryer. I can also see that in two days, 112 pounds are due. This is a very manageable amount. Based on this, these orders shouldn't be difficult to finish. I have seen it happen when everyone decides to drop off at once. Let's say an attendant texts me and says, "We got a lot of drop-offs." What exactly does that mean? Maybe someone has just returned from vacation and dropped off 110 pounds, and a new customer walked in with seventy-five more. That's on top of the 225 we already have in the system. Now I have the information to decide whether I should bring in extra help in the next day or two.

I can then go to the next screen and see what still needs to be picked up by customers, whether they have paid, and how old their order is. The previous owner didn't ask customers to prepay for their drop-offs, and I decided to keep that policy in place (depending on your customer base, you might decide to have them pay when they drop off their clothes). If anything is "too old," we can send the customer a text reminder from the POS, or an attendant will call. You might be surprised that sometimes prepaid items hit this list. While I'm glad we got paid, I'd still rather not have to store customers' items for six months.

The next thing I can do is look at the driver's schedule for the upcoming days. This helps me again to gauge how busy we will be. We do pickups and deliveries Monday through Friday, between 8 AM and 1 PM. We have several recurring customers that are scheduled every other Monday, so every other Monday is usually our heaviest day. Again, I can use this information to help me schedule my staff. The system also sets up what it thinks is the most efficient driver schedule for the route.

So far, anyone at the laundromat can access all the information I've mentioned. I haven't even gotten to the owner's reports. In the system I use, these can only be seen with the owner's access.

Monthly and YTD pounds washed. You need to know how much laundry you're processing and be able to compare it with other years.

Total number of orders and average price per order. Is the business growing, or are there other factors involved? Obviously, you can see if total sales are up or down, but what's driving that? Did you add a large commercial account, and your drop-off customers are down? Do you service the same number of customers, but have higher revenue because of a price increase?

Services and service options sold. This is where I can see what we sold and at what price points. For example, we had different price points for Wash & Fold throughout the year. One or two because we made errors initially and another because we raised prices during the year. This is how I know how many blankets and pet beds we processed. I also realized we were missing an opportunity at the register by not upselling customers from our house detergent to premium brands like Gain, Tide, or Unstoppables. Many times, If you simply ask customers if they want Tide, they'll say yes because it's a familiar brand.

View promotion usage and lists of customers who used them. Are customers responding to your promotions? If we give out coupons at certain town events, we can see how many are redeemed and consider whether it's worth attending those events in the future.

List of new and recurring customers. The question I have all attendants ask when we get a new customer is, "How did they find us?" Was it a Google search or a referral? Do they drive past us every day?

Monthly customer revenue. This shows you how much each customer spent and the last time they used our services. When I go through this report, I can find customers who used to come in every month and then just stopped. Now I can contact that customer and offer them a deal to get them back.

Prospective Pickup & Delivery customers. This is a list of customers who went to the website and filled out information but never placed an order. I can also reach out to them.

Reengage customer list. This is a list of people who previously did Pickup & Delivery but don't anymore. Sometimes, customers do Pickup for a special reason and aren't long-term customers. Maybe they had surgery and won't continue it when they're better. Sometimes, they just stop, and we don't know why. We can reach back out to them, too.

Customer list. This is a list of every customer we have in the system, and it can be exported to an Excel spreadsheet.

Employee reconciliation. It reconciles cash and tracks all transactions during a shift.

Employee gratuities. People do love their tips, and it's important to track them to make sure employees get paid correctly.

Inventory snapshot. You can view current inventory counts and reorder thresholds.

Cash events. View a list of all cash events, including purchases and refunds. This is good for when you might not be in the store often.

Product sales. This gives you a look at sales of behind-the-counter items such as Tide pods, bottles of detergent, fabric sheets, etc.

Turns per machine. Turns refers to how many times customers use a machine per day. This will let you know how frequently each machine is being used and if there is increased usage. It can also tell you what machines are currently in use. One reason you might want to know turns is if you decide to add equipment or remove equipment. If your twenty-pound washers average 1.9 turns per day, your forty-pounders 3.1, and your sixty-pounders 2.9, you can make an informed decision. At the very least, you wouldn't add more twenty-pounders, and you might even remove some to make space for larger machines because that is what your customers are using.

Another great thing about a laundry POS system is that the companies that host your POS will also develop your website. Some let you customize your website with different templates, but the important thing is that they do it for you. I say it more than once in this book: half of laundromats don't even have a website. Getting one professionally done is one less thing you must worry about. They also do the SEO (search engine optimization) for you so local customers can find you. If you're curious about what mine looks like, take a look! www.washingwell.biz.

Some POS systems have fully integrated payroll. Employees can clock in and out at the register, and the system sends the information to the payroll processing company. They also allow you to work with DoorDash, Uber, Lyft, and any other companies in the gig economy that do pickups and deliveries (I'll talk more about Pickup & Delivery in its own chapter).

I'm sure if I had one of the reps for these companies write this section, they would add fifty other things these systems can do, but I think you can see how valuable a POS system can be. Especially if you want to grow your business.

Now, from the customer's perspective.

Customers expect technology. It's part of all our lives. You can sit on your couch and run your life from your phone. You can order food, medicine, groceries, do your banking, have your doctor's visit, and in New Jersey, even order alcohol and never leave your living room. So why are laundromats different? You'd be shocked if you needed to rent a car and Avis didn't have a website. With many laundromats, you can't even find out what their hours are. If you order a slice of pizza, they have a POS system. Go into a hair salon and set an appointment; they don't write it down anymore; they put you in the computer. Laundromats look like relics from the past, especially without a basic website.

Now, forget everything I told you about running the business for a minute and just think about what it would be like if you were the customer. If you used a laundromat regularly and they had an app that could tell you how many machines were currently in use so you know if the size machine you need is available, wouldn't that be useful to you? What if they had a rewards program on the app, and you could get free items based on your usage? Say you drop off your clothes for Wash & Fold and are told it will be done by Wednesday at 6 PM, but they get it done early; they can send you a text message that your clothes are ready for you to pick up Tuesday at 3 PM. As a Pickup & Delivery customer, you would get a text when the driver is on their way to your house, and another one when they either picked up or dropped off your clothes.

In 2024, these aren't just nice things to have. They are the *baseline* expectations of all consumers when shopping for any product or service they need.

If you need a last reason to get a POS system, I assume most owners will want to sell the business at some point. This will help the prospective buyer do their due diligence. The laundry business is still mostly a cash business. I had one gentleman tell me it's the only business left that you still pay in quarters. You will have a much easier time building trust with the buyer because verifying everything you're doing is so much easier with POS. All this information will be extremely valuable to a new owner. The easier you make their transition and the more information they have, the more valuable your business will be to them. Even if all your numbers are 100 percent accurate, a new owner who wants to scale the business up still has a lot of work ahead of them because they know the topline number, for example $400,000 in sales, but not exactly how the number was reached. How much of that was from blankets? Minimum fees? Tide pods? They can't truly dig into the numbers until they create their own with a new POS.

Running Your Laundromat

"Train people well enough so they can leave. Treat them well
enough so they don't want to."
—Richard Branson

"Be a yardstick of quality. Some people aren't used to an
environment where excellence is expected."
—Steve Jobs

The first place to start with running your laundromat is having the right staff. Unfortunately, there is no silver bullet for finding or hiring employees. It's hard work, and you're competing against major corporations for the same work pool. I suggest that having a deep "well" will help you attract better talent. I don't mean a water well, but instead, pay well. Train them well. Treat them well.

One of the biggest decisions a small business can make is hiring or firing employees. If Target hires someone who doesn't work out, it's not a big deal. They were one of a hundred thousand employees. If you have a staff of two and hire the wrong person, it can greatly impact your business. On a small staff, one person can make or break your business, especially if you aren't going to be at your store on a full-time basis.

When I bought my store, it had two employees that we were keeping. We still have one of them, and she's fantastic. I've never heard a bad word about her, and customers love her. She folds like a dynamo, is never late, and constantly works. I know I'm very lucky to have her, and I'm glad she likes working for us.

The other employee didn't work out so well, and I fired her within three months of taking over the store. I quickly realized she talked a good game but let the other employee do most of the work. She called out sick a lot, fell asleep on the couch by the front door, and once closed the store so she could go get ice cream. She watched more Netflix on my account at the store than my whole family did.

After I fired her, I started hearing customer stories and knew I'd made the right decision. People felt uncomfortable just asking her for change. I heard that she told a customer to go to another laundromat. There was plenty more, but you get the point. I might never know if she permanently drove any customers away, but I did have people tell me they sometimes didn't come in when she was there.

As a small business owner, I know how hard it is to find good employees, but just like with due diligence, don't rush the hiring process. And like due diligence, I know this part of the business is no fun, but considering the stakes of hiring the wrong person, it's worth taking your time to do it right. If you hire the first available person, you're taking a gamble. The other side of this problem is if you do hire the wrong person, are you willing to fire them? I've seen many times in places I've worked where the wrong employee just wreaked havoc with the team, but the higher-ups or HR were unwilling to do their job and fire the person. In this case, you're both the higher-ups and HR.

In employees, I look for friendliness and a willingness to help the customer. You can teach anyone to fold and use a register, but only some are good with customers. A friendly or unfriendly attendant can make or break the customer's experience, especially since laundromats are only so big. Unless the customer leaves, it's hard to avoid that employee. I also recommend getting references and doing a background check. A background check isn't expensive, and it's important since the employee will deal with cash and credit cards without much oversight. Sometimes, just Googling a person will yield interesting results. Before we fired that attendant, we googled her and found out about her prison sentence and the crimes she pled guilty to. After reading that, we started to fill in some of the pieces to her puzzle.

Going back to the three "wells," the first one is to pay well. Depending on what part of the country you're in, the actual dollar amount will vary, but you should pay the going rate. One advantage you might have over

Walmart and McDonald's is that many customers tip for Wash & Fold. When you add that to the going wage, employees can often make much more percentage-wise working for you than they could working for these larger companies. That will help even out some of the things you might not be able to offer, like vacation pay. You could also offer performance incentives. For example, if the store hits $25,000 in sales for the month, each employee gets an extra $200 bonus. This way, they have an incentive for the store to do well beyond having enough money for their check to clear. Maybe you offer a $25 gift card if a customer leaves a positive review and names them. Remember that each state has different laws about "sick" time, but if you have to pay it anyway, you might as well include it as a benefit.

The second "well" is to train them well. Some larger laundromats, or those with several stores, have formal training programs, but most don't. That doesn't mean they have to get haphazard training, and if I were interviewing someone, I would tell them exactly how we'd train them. I'm sure many people applying to work at a laundry think there is nothing to do but watch TV and answer simple questions or, on the other end of the spectrum, that they will be tossed into the store to either sink or swim on their own.

I developed a checklist of everything they would need to know to work in the store, from logging onto the computer to how to wash and fold. I don't use a set amount of time for how long training is, say one week, because some people catch on quicker than others. So, I will schedule Chris, our new hire, to open with Sue. They then use the checklist and review as many items as possible, as long as they can cover them well. The next time, Chris will close with Janet, and they'll review the night part of the checklist. Then, he'll work with Sue again to review what they have covered and whatever remains on the checklist.

During this time, I will also check in with the new hire and answer any questions that Sue or Janet couldn't answer or expand on topics a little more. They will also get trained on the register, but they can do this at home, and I'll pay them for that time. The POS systems today have training videos you can watch and learn from, so as long as the employee can log on, they can do it from anywhere.

When I think they're ready—and that depends on the employee—I will go through the entire checklist with them. If they need a little more time, I'll schedule them with someone else to work on what they still need. If they are ready, I will "baby step" them to working alone. Most laundromats are not busy enough to have multiple people working, so employees must know they'll be alone. I would schedule Chris for a four-hour shift, sandwiched between the opener and closer. So Chris will spend an hour working with Sue, and she will make sure he is set up on the register and knows what he is doing next for Wash & Fold. He will then work two hours by himself and overlap for an hour with Janet when she comes in. She can answer any questions he might have and ensure he knows how to count out his register. If that goes well, maybe the next time he works, he'll be alone for three hours until he says he can do the shift alone. I'm also just a phone call away if there is anything another employee can't answer for him.

The third "well" seems so obvious that it shouldn't need to be mentioned, but it is. Treat them well. I'm sure you've had jobs where you were treated like crap but then expected to treat the customers like "gold." I've never understood how companies and managers think this will work. If you take care of your employees, they'll care for your customers. Show your employees respect and kindness; they will pass that on to the customers. Treat them poorly, and they'll take it out on the customer.

When it comes to making the customer happy, I give my staff a wide latitude. If a customer isn't happy with something, I tell my employees to just take care of them. The only exception is if the customer crosses the line. Life's too short to be cursed at, or worse. Fortunately, most customers don't go there. They save that for the airlines. If it means giving them a free wash, even if they made the mistake, just give them the wash. If they need fifty cents for the dryer, give it to them.

For me, this does two things. First, I look at the lifetime value of the customer. Some customers spend thousands of dollars in a laundromat over time. Do I want to argue with them over a five-dollar wash? Even if I win the argument, I'll lose the war anyway because they'll go somewhere else, tell someone else, or leave the dreaded bad review. Secondly, this empowers the staff to take ownership. I honestly don't want a text or phone call at home asking if they can give someone money for another wash. They all know to just take care of it.

If it's the customer's fault, I try to use that as a teaching moment and to build some goodwill. For example, those little bottles of detergent you get at the dollar store are good for five loads. We've had people pour the whole bottle in for one load. You can imagine their clothes don't come out of the wash like they would like them to. This is when we politely tell them they used too much soap and how much to use next time. Then we tell them we'll rewash it for them with our quarters. Sometimes, they say they will pay, but we still pay for it. Now they know how much to use next time, but we also bought ourselves some goodwill. The message is, *You can come to us because we'll take care of you.*

Sometimes, it's our fault. If we make a mistake, we own it and fix it. Again, you can argue or make excuses, but to what end? I had one lady just trying to wash a comforter, and we had problems with the water pressure in the building, and that morning was a mess. Long story short, it didn't go through the rinse cycle, and the comforter was sopping wet. I told her to give me her phone number and address and that we would pay to dry it and deliver it to her that night. I wasn't going to make her wait around for us to get the situation straightened out.

I expect every customer to be greeted on their way in and get some kind of goodbye on their way out. If I had a bigger store where the attendant might not see a customer walk in, I would have the attendant greet them and offer help as soon as they realized it.

The store has to be clean. This is non-negotiable. How can you run a service that cleans clothes for a living and then have a dirty store? There should be a daily and weekly cleaning schedule. You also want the store to be well-lit. A well-lit store sets an inviting mood for the customer. It's also important at night. Some customers might not feel as safe coming to the laundromat when it's dark outside, and if it's dark and dingy inside, they might just go to a competitor with no competitive advantage other than brighter lighting.

When I worked in a grocery store, we always stressed cleanliness in all the areas a customer would go to. For example, if the bathroom is dirty, and the employees use the same restroom as the customers, it's reasonable that the customer might question how much care the employees are giving to handling their food. It's the same with laundromats. One of the biggest complaints about laundries is that they are dirty. If the customer is bringing you their clothes to make cleaner, and they walk into a dirty store, how can they have confidence you'll get their clothes clean?

When it comes to the store's decor and what you play on the TV, I like to play it very safe, or to put it more bluntly, boring. Customers coming into the store are your guests, and the host's job is to make their guests feel welcome and comfortable. When I checked out that baseball facility I mentioned earlier, the owner had on what most people would consider a very fringe political show. I mentioned that to the broker and said I could see that turning people off. The broker didn't like that and asked what I thought he should put on. I told him that baseball has its own network, so why not start there? This is why when you go into any doctor's waiting room with a TV, it's either a cooking show or one about people buying a house. I don't care what someone watches at home, but they should put something on for the customer in the store. It's the same with movies. I wouldn't put an R-rated movie on Netflix in case a five-year-old walks in with their parent.

Keep politics and religion out of it. Support, donate, and vote for whomever you like in your private life, but leave it out of the store. People come to a laundromat to clean their clothes. That's it.

Customer Service

"There is only one boss—the customer. And he can fire everybody in the company from the chairman on down, simply by spending his money somewhere else."
—Sam Walton, Walmart's founder

I've always felt that 75 percent of customer service is just being nice. It's such a simple concept. As a customer, if you have a cashier screw up, but they're nice, sincere, and apologetic, you normally give them the benefit of the doubt. It's hard to get mad at someone who's nice to you. But being friendly only gets you so far. There's still a 25 percent gap. Here are some ways to close that gap.

Don't assume you're giving great customer service just because you, the owner, are there. When I used to sell mystery shopping services and spoke with small business owners, they would always agree that the service was bad, but they usually never thought of themselves as possibly giving bad service. This is a common trap for small businesses.

I remember going to a small hobby shop in town. I had been there before and was unimpressed, but decided to give it another chance. I walked in, waited to be acknowledged for about two minutes, and walked out. I left a one-star review on Google. I was surprised that I received a reply because they had several other bad reviews that weren't addressed. In not-the-nicest response, the owner said they greeted everyone and questioned my idea of service. The owner was there when I went in and was one of the people who couldn't be bothered to acknowledge me. If this owner were interviewed, I'm sure he would mention how good their service was even though several of the one-star reviews specifically mentioned him.

A mistake I see laundromats make is they only talk to regulars. I don't mystery shop my competitors, but I will go to other laundromats to see what they are doing and learn from them. Almost without fail, I won't get acknowledged unless I try to seek out an attendant. They get caught in the trap of speaking to regulars, so they feel like they talk to customers and have a good relationship with them. Unfortunately, the person coming in to do their laundry for the first time doesn't seem to get that same customer service. My store has the Wash & Fold area next to the register so we can greet everyone as they walk in.

This segues into my next point about the deadliest customer to a business, the silent customer. They are the "reverse Karens." They don't complain or ask to speak to the owner. They smile on their way out and wish you a nice day. But they didn't have a good experience and aren't returning. According to a PeopleMetrics survey, one out of every four customers will not tell you if they have experienced a problem. If you have attendants who don't talk to customers, that number is probably higher, and you'll never know it.

That's why customer complaints are good. Many owners think that a lack of complaints means everything is good. They aren't taking into account the silent customer, so they live in a bit of a naive state that everything is fantastic. The great thing about complaints is that we know not everything is perfect, and if a customer is complaining, it gives us a chance to fix it and hopefully stop that customer from going elsewhere. There's also a good chance that if it's a legitimate complaint, it might have bothered other customers, too.

Customer service doesn't have to be hard for a laundromat, but I haven't come across one yet with a perfect five-star Google rating, including my own. If you remember the basics, you can eliminate most of the complaints. Be friendly. People like nice people. Train your employees so they feel comfortable engaging with your customers. If your attendants are scared that someone might ask them a question (because they haven't been trained), I don't blame them for not socializing with customers. And lastly, educate your customers on how to use a laundromat so they get the best experience. We've all seen the customer that is struggling to figure out what to do because they've never been to a laundromat before. Go over and help them, and you'll instantly win them over.

Educating your customers is a great way to help prevent situations before they happen. We have signs up to tell the customer how much detergent they should use in the machines. Customers are usually fifty-fifty when it comes to using too much soap. Half apologize and the other half blame the washing machine. Many people don't read the signs, but if we can prevent some people from using too much detergent, it can help prevent situations like this.

When we see new self-serve customers come in with blankets, we inform them that the washers all have a blanket setting. If someone brings us a Wash & Fold item that is dry clean only, we'll ask them if they still want us to wash it. Sometimes, the customers don't realize that it's dry clean only, and sometimes, they don't care. At least if we ask them ahead of time, they have less cause to complain if it doesn't come out well.

Equipment

Discussing laundry equipment is much like discussing cars. There are so many makes and models of cars you could write a book about just one type. The same goes for laundry equipment, so I'll just give you an overview. When the time comes that you're looking for new or refurbished equipment, it would be best for you to talk to several distributors to see what they offer.

To start with, there is no perfect ratio of machines needed. It is inaccurate to say you need X amount of sixty-pounders, Y amount of forty-pounders, Z amount of thirty-pounders, etc. The right mix depends entirely on your particular store. If you have a small store, you might not have the space to add many larger machines.

What does your competition have? There is a trend in the industry toward larger machines because it allows people to do more laundry at once. What are the demographics of your area? If you are surrounded mostly by families, then your mix would probably lean toward bigger machines more so than if you are in an area with more retirees.

What is the makeup of your business? For example, when I bought my store, my first thought was that I needed to buy bigger machines. Over time, I realized that my business is more geared toward Wash & Fold. If I added larger machines, it wouldn't really change the self-service part of the business.

Next, what types of machines will you put in your stores? There are two types of washers. Top-load washers and front-load washers. Top-load washers are what most people are used to because that's what you'd most likely have in a house, condo, or apartment. These aren't popular options for laundromat owners; you can go to many laundromats and not even find one. They are less expensive but use more water and can be rougher on clothes. They also have less capacity than front loaders and are easier for customers to try and over-fill, which can lead to a broken machine. They have a lifespan of ten to twelve years. I had a few at my laundromat and took them out to make more space. I'm not exaggerating when I say they were almost never used.

Front loaders range in size from twenty-pound capacity up to two hundred-pound capacity. You won't see a two hundred-pounder in a laundromat, but I just wanted to give you an idea of how big they can get. (These types of machines can be found in institutions that do their own laundry, such as hospitals and prisons.) Front loaders are more expensive than top loaders, but otherwise, they are superior in every way. They are more water- and energy-efficient, gentler on clothes, and more effective at cleaning them. They also have a longer average life span (between thirteen and fifteen years) and many additional machine options.

Another consideration is soft- versus hard-mount washers. Hard-mount machines don't have a suspension system and are mounted directly to the floor. They're good when the laundromat has solid and stable flooring supporting their weight. Soft-mount machines come equipped with a suspension system, preventing the transmission of excessive vibration to the floor. These are good for placement over basements or other sensitive areas.

As with anything, both types have their pros and cons. For a soft-mount machine, you just need a level floor that can support the machine's weight. They run at higher extraction speeds (i.e., they spin faster), which helps the machine to remove more water and allows the clothes to dry quicker. They can also be installed as close to the wall as you can put them and are easier to lift and pull away from the wall for maintenance. The downside of soft-mount machines is they generally cost 10–20 percent more than hard-mount because there are more parts. Also, all the springs and shocks inside the machine make it larger than hard-mount machines and may take up more valuable real estate inside your laundromat.

I'm not discussing all these machines' specific options because there are just far too many. I will say that today's machines make gathering information about your business much easier, in addition to the obvious benefits of being more efficient and less costly to run. This is why you should befriend some distributors when you're ready.

Stack dryers are exactly what they sound like. They consist of two dryers in one unit, one above the other. These are very common in laundromats because of the space savings. They cost more than single-load dryers, but they offer double the capacity. Gas dryers are more common and usually more energy efficient than electric ones. In most laundromats, you'll see a ratio very close to one dryer per washing machine. People have a tendency to overload washers and underfill the dryers. Dryers have an average lifespan of ten to fifteen years. In addition to stack dryers, there are also large capacity fifty- and seventy-five-pound single units.

There aren't too many laundromats that use folding machines, but I wanted to make you aware of them. You need to have both the space and enough Wash & Fold business to make the machine worthwhile, and most laundries aren't at that level. A folding machine does exactly what it sounds like. The advantage is that it can fold large amounts of laundry quicker than a human, allowing the owner to use less labor.

As with any type of equipment, regular maintenance is crucial to getting more life out of it. Read the manual and understand what you can do to maintain your equipment's lifespan.

Know Your Competition

"Goodwill is the one and only asset that competition cannot
undersell or destroy."
—Ludwig Borne

"Competition is always a good thing. It forces us to do our best.
A monopoly rends people complacent and satisfied with
mediocrity."—Nancy Pearcey

I like to keep an eye on the competition, both online and in person. I hope they aren't doing it back to me, but they should be. I do know one laundromat nearby that follows us on Instagram, and we follow them back. According to a survey by *American Coin-Op* in their November 2023 issue, 93 percent of store owners surveyed said they scope out the competition.

When I check out their online presence, it's very easy. I look at their most recent reviews and see what customers say about them. One laundromat was bought about a year ago, and I've watched their reviews get more positive, so the new owner is moving in the right direction. I will check out their website and compare their prices with mine. I also want to know if they are doing anything new. Did they add a service? Did they raise their prices? Are they offering any new promotions? If they have an email or text list, I'll sign up for that.

I also go into their stores. I take real laundry or some old towels and throw them in the dryer for twenty minutes. This gives me enough time just to walk around. I look at both the physical parts of the store and the atmosphere.

For the physical aspect, I'm looking at how many machines they have, the mix of machines, and what they're charging. Half of laundromats don't have websites and even fewer list their prices, so sometimes, this is the only way to find out what they're charging. I want to see how many machines, if any, are out of order. Anyone can have a machine down if they are waiting for a repair person or a part, but having too many "out of order" signs doesn't look good. I'll use the bathroom and see if it's clean and stocked.

If they do Wash & Fold, are they using a POS system and electric scale or writing orders by hand? How much Wash & Fold can I see (sometimes a laundry might have a back room, so you won't be able to see it)? Does it look like the machines are well-maintained? Is the store clean? What amenities do they have? TVs? Seating? Do they have soap dispensers and soda and candy machines? Do they have anything else to generate revenue, like a massage chair, ATM, or video games?

For the atmosphere, I want to know how the customer feels in the store. First and foremost, is the attendant friendly and welcoming? I have a small store, so we can easily greet everyone as they walk in or go to a machine. You often find that the attendant talks to the regulars and doesn't talk to anyone they don't know. I want to see if the store is nice and brightly lit or dark and dingy. Do they have the TV or music on? Do they have comfortable seating? I really want to know if this is a place I'd mind hanging out in for over an hour while I do my laundry.

You might be surprised that I don't look to see if the store is busy or not. Customer flow is very hard to predict. I've seen in my store times when every dryer is being used, and an hour later, the store is empty. So, looking at the store at any given moment won't tell you how well it's doing.

After my visits, I do what is called a SWOT analysis. If you haven't heard of it, it stands for Strengths, Weaknesses, Opportunities, and Threats. It's very straightforward for a laundromat. It can get more complicated for a more complex business, but we'll keep it simple. You should have done a less formal version of this during your due diligence. I saved this part until now because once you own the business, you'll better understand your strengths and weaknesses. To quote Roy L. Smith, "The successful man is the one who finds out what is the matter with his business before his competitors do." As an example, I'll do a SWOT on my store and compare it to the five closest stores.

Strengths. What do we do well?

The two things I strive for are cleanliness and friendliness.

Our prices are in line with the market.

Weaknesses. What could we improve?

Our store is physically small. I just don't have the room to add bigger machines or expand. I'm maxed out on products I can sell because of our size.

Opportunities

We've just scratched the surface with Pickup & Delivery for residential and commercial accounts. We could grow the business much quicker by adding more commercial accounts.

Threats

Right now, only one laundromat in our area besides us offers Pickup & Delivery. If more stores get into Pickup & Delivery, we could be vying for the same customers.

Pickup & Delivery is an opportunity for the entire industry. I need to figure out how to best take advantage of that opportunity based on my store's location and the surrounding demographics.

What I want to take away from these visits is what it's like to be a customer at their laundromats. Where do I need to raise my game to compete with them? Even if I think we're better overall, there's usually something that they are better at that my store can start doing. I also want to know their prices. If I think we're just as good as them—if not better— and they're charging more, then I have room to raise my prices.

According to the same *American Coin-Op* survey, owners felt the two most effective ways to fend off competition were cleanliness and customer service (32 percent and 29 percent, respectively). Pricing was only at 7 percent. If you offer value, the price usually takes care of itself.

Regarding competition, I like to live by the words of Andy Grove's book title (co-founder of Intel), *Only the Paranoid Survive*. When you stop to pat yourself on the back for the good job you're doing, that's when you get complacent; your competition speeds right by you, and you're left wondering what happened.

Marketing Your Business

In today's world, there are many ways to market your business both digitally and with more old-school techniques. Both can be very effective, and you must determine what works best for you. I've found that most laundromats stick with one or the other approach. Some owners fully embrace technology with SEO, Facebook, and Google Ads. Others don't even have a website.

I'm going to give you *sixteen* different ways to promote your business. Some may work for you, and some may not. I recommend that whatever marketing initiative you choose, you own it. I believe in the "inch wide, mile deep" philosophy. Don't be on ten social media platforms and do them all poorly. Pick one or two that you can just rock. These are listed in no particular order because you need to do what works for your situation.

Website

According to the 2023 CLA laundry industry survey, only 53 percent of laundromats have websites. I'm not sure how that is even possible, but when I google laundromats in certain areas, it does appear that most don't have one. I think in 2024, it is a must. The great thing is that it doesn't have to be fancy or expensive. You can use GoDaddy to create a basic website for almost nothing. You're not doing e-commerce through your website, so a few simple pages with pictures are all you need. Have an "About Us" page that personalizes your store. Ben and J. Lo started Happy Suds when they saw a need (and why not? We've seen Ben doing the drive-up at Dunkin' Donuts). List your hours, services and prices. List your address, phone number, and email address. Add a few pictures of the outside and inside of the store and maybe happy people doing laundry, and boom, you're done. You have a website. It doesn't need to win any awards or have bells and whistles. You just need something simple to give customers in your area basic information.

Final analysis: Low cost and easy to do.

Billboards

The good old reliable side-of-the-road billboard. I inquired about one close to my store, but it was already under contract. I thought this would be a great way to promote our Wash & Fold and Pickup & Delivery services. A billboard gives great visibility, and I don't recall ever seeing a laundromat with one, so it would stand out. This was the old-fashioned kind of billboard with the same picture on it for six months. They also have electronic ones. To give you an idea of the cost, it was $1800 monthly for six months, plus set-up costs.

Final Analysis: Easy to set up (the company will design it for you) but pricey for a laundromat.

Chamber of Commerce

The Chamber is an often-forgotten way to get more business and grow your community presence, but you must work at it. It's like a gym. If you get a membership but never go, you'll think it was a waste of money. If you don't participate, you won't get anything out of it. In my first year in the Chamber, we hosted a ribbon cutting as the new owners, which many Chamber members attended and helped to promote. We also held a networking function, which cost us zero dollars. The chamber promoted it, and I got another Chamber member to donate the food. I don't expect every Chamber member to bring me their laundry, but I want to be at the top of their mind if they need our service. They may also be able to connect us with a customer or business that needs us.

Final analysis: You need to put in the work, but the cost is usually only $100 to $300, depending on where you are.

Facebook, Instagram, and Google Ads

These can all be effective, but it might be a good idea to get professional help before spending a lot of money on different platforms. They're easy to set up yourself, but it's also easy to waste money by not running the right ads, using the best keywords, or not targeting your audience. I heard on a webinar about one laundromat owner who spent $10,000 on these ads and got a handful of customers. They would have been better off using some of that to hire a professional.

One thing to consider is what type of ad you want. Do you want to include videos, image-based, carousel, etc.? You also need to be highly targeted. I typed "laundromat" as an experiment on one social media site. I did it several times, and not once did I see an ad with a laundromat near my house. Some weren't even in my state. If I had clicked on any of them, it would have been wasted money for that store. They probably paid good money for the word "laundromat," but a store in Atlanta doesn't want to be found by someone in New Jersey. A third thing to consider is where your customers will most likely find you. For example, Google ads are usually better for the "ready to buy" customer, while Facebook is more passive.

Ultimately, you'll decide if the campaign was worth it, but two metrics that can help you are "return on ad spend" and "customer lifetime value." The return on ad spend measures the revenue generated for every dollar spent on advertising. It wouldn't be a profitable campaign if the revenue created wasn't higher than the ad spend. The customer lifetime value measures the long-term value of acquired customers. For example, maybe you spend $1000 and attract only one customer, but that customer spends a consistent fifty dollars a week in your store. If that customer spends $2600 a year, you still double your money, even if you would have liked to have generated more traffic with that ad.

Final analysis: If done right, ads can help you generate increased revenue. If done poorly, they can be a money pit.

Facebook, Instagram, and LinkedIn Accounts

Nothing says you have to pay to be on social media. Having an account and setting up a page for your business is free. You can actively promote your business, and you can also be a part of local community groups. Almost every town of any size has a Facebook page. If you do engage, don't be that person who just posts every day about their laundromat. After a while, it will turn people off. It's fine to talk about your business, but have something constructive to add to a conversation. I included LinkedIn because it's a great way to connect with other laundromat owners and those in the business. Just realize you will get zero customers through LinkedIn.

Final analysis: It's free and has nothing but upside potential

Advertising Around Town

Some companies specialize in putting your ads in unique places around town. Think of the advertisements on shopping carts and benches. It seems like I see my real estate agent at every bus stop I pass in town.

These companies also sell the ads on the back of grocery store coupons. The great thing is that you would only be paired up with a store that's close to you, and you can put your coupon or call to action on the receipt.

Final analysis: The ads around town are more for brand recognition, which could be expensive. The receipts are a good way to get coupons into the hands of people who might not normally use a laundromat.

Door Hangers

I know they are so 1990s, but if you open your door, you at least see the information about my laundromat. When we get a new Pickup & Delivery customer, we put them on nearby houses or apartments. If one house on the street can afford it, there's a good chance their neighbors can, too. You don't need to do Pickup & Delivery for door hangers. You can pick out a neighborhood or apartment complex and just put them out. I recently had some printed, and they were about twelve cents each. You could do a hundred apartments for twelve dollars and up your step count at the same time.

Final analysis: They are inexpensive, and you're at least guaranteed that they'll see it.

Start a Referral Program

Referral programs are great because other people do the work for you. A great way to do it is to print simple business cards that explain the program and give several to your Wash & Fold and Pickup & Delivery customers. Every time a new customer uses the card, they get 10 percent or a fixed dollar amount off their order, and the person who referred them also gets a discount for their next order. You can make it so that it's only good for the first time a new customer uses it, but a person can refer as many new customers as they want and get a discount each time.

Final analysis: You can't lose. If no one refers anyone, it costs you a few business cards, and if you get a referral, it doesn't cost you much to acquire that new customer.

Cross-promote with a Local Business

This is another inexpensive way to get the word out, and you don't see it very often. Let's say there's a pizza place in your strip mall. You could hand out flyers or leave coupons for your customers to take, and they can, in return, tape your flyer to their pizza boxes. There's no reason you couldn't do this with any small business in your area.

Final analysis: Easy and inexpensive to do. There's no downside.

Newspaper Ads

Unfortunately, newspapers aren't what they once were, but most towns still have a little local paper. It has a lot of ads, a letter from the mayor, some news on the high school, dates for recycling, etc. I have one town paper delivered to my store, and I get a different one for my house. I do see laundromats advertised in these. When we were having our ribbon cutting, I advertised in the paper. The hard thing about an ad is that it is difficult to gauge the return on investment unless you have a call to action that is specific to the ad, like a coupon. You won't know if that new customer saw the ad or came to you because they drove past and noticed you.

Final analysis: An ad will cost several hundred dollars a month, and you'll probably be required to run it for a set amount of time, so it can get expensive.

Do Something for Charity

There's a lot you can do here. If you're in the area of a homeless shelter, you could offer to do free laundry. You could have a coat or clothing drive. The Coin Laundry Association also has its own charity, The Laundry Cares Foundation, where they host Free Laundry and Literacy Day events in different cities nationwide.

Final analysis: There's only upside in helping the community where your business is located.

Online Reviews

You might not think of online reviews as marketing, but they are often the first thing a customer will see about your store. They google "laundromat" in a certain area, and two pop up. One store has a 4.6 rating, and is a mile away. The other has a 3.6 rating and is also a mile away. Which would you choose? You're going to pick the higher-rated one first. Sometimes, online reviews can be unfair because anyone can write anything, but that's life. You need to be proactive with reviews. When you get one, always respond positively to them. If you fight with a customer and tell them they're wrong, it might make you feel good at the time, but it looks bad when customers see your attitude. You might be correct, but it can come off as aggressive or rude to someone reading the review.

You can also ask your customers to leave reviews. Unfortunately, life sometimes gets in the way, and they forget or never get around to it. It's OK to give them a little incentive. I put a sign up in my store that the first five customers who leave a Google review get a free Washing Well laundry bag. We sell those for $12, so it's a nice incentive. I got our five reviews in a weekend. This stays between you and me, but you can also write reviews about yourself. All three of my kids have left five-star reviews.

Final analysis: It's free, and people will write what they want to anyway, so you should stay on top of it.

Direct Mail

It's an oldie but still a goodie. With emails and texts, people forget about mail. Emails can easily be deleted without even being opened, but if you got a handwritten envelope delivered to your house or business with a stamp, wouldn't you open it? Of course, you would. The whole challenge with marketing is getting the customer to see your offer. If they open the envelope, mission accomplished.

The second part is what's in your letter. If you're not a writer, don't worry because the fewer words you use, the better. If it's a dense letter, they won't read it. When I write to businesses, I start with "Got Laundry?"

in large bold font and center it. I then say take that chore off your hands. We'll pick it up, wash and fold it, and bring it back to you. Then, I mention some businesses we already work with, like physical therapists, gyms, funeral homes, etc. That's it. That's the whole letter. Short and to the point. You might want to start by targeting certain types of businesses, such as physical therapists, in a five-mile radius around your store.

I do a similar letter for residential customers. The same "Got Laundry?" is centered and in large bold font. I list everything we offer. Wash & Fold. Pickup & Delivery. Friendly staff. Two TVs and the NFL Ticket. Air conditioning. Snack machine. I would also include a call to action. Bring this letter in for five dollars off blankets or five dollars off your first Wash & Fold.

Getting the addresses is easy because you can google the businesses. For homeowners, I used Zillow. Let's say you have identified customers living in a house valued over $500,000 as your target market for Wash & Fold or Pickup & Delivery. You can use Zillow to target those addresses. You won't get the customers' names, but you can identify an area you want to target and get all the addresses. You can also do a mailing to an apartment complex and slightly reword it and maybe change the offer to gear it toward self-serve customers.

Final analysis: Stamps are a little expensive but it's a great way to get your message seen.

Email Marketing

So, I just got done telling you how easy it is to delete emails, but that is mostly the case when they are unsolicited. People will open the letter out of curiosity and ignore the email unless you have a list of people who have opted in for your email list.

If you ask your customers for their email, it could be a great way to communicate with them. Not only can you send them promotions, but you can also send them informational emails, such as how often certain clothes need to be washed or what all the symbols mean on clothes tags. It's also an easy way to let them know if you will close early on Christmas Eve or if you might open late because of a snowstorm.

Final analysis: It's inexpensive to use an email service like Constant Contact; just make sure the customer has opted in to receive them.

Knock on Doors

This is another old-fashioned technique that's not used anymore in our digital age, but it can be very effective. You sent letters to ten physical therapists and didn't hear anything back. Go visit them in person. They're all close to your store, otherwise you wouldn't have sent them letters in the first place.

Just go in and introduce yourself. "Hi. I'm Jennifer. I own the Missing Sock Laundromat on Main Street. I was curious: how do you wash all your towels?" Then, let the conversation take its natural course. You can even try to sell the person you're talking to. They obviously work close to your store. Maybe they'd want to drop off their laundry before work and pick it up on the way home.

Final analysis: It's free, but it is sales, so you have to be up for it.

Town Celebrations

Many towns have a "Day" with vendors, food, music, etc. The whole family often attends these events. The town I live in has one, and where I grew up has a Labor Day parade, which is a big event. Our laundromat happens to straddle two towns, so we attended both their days and gave out coupons. I'll talk to anyone, but I specifically looked for families with kids, and if they had a stroller, it was a bonus. Kids mean lots of laundry, and parents make for good Wash & Fold prospects. The cost for both days was $200.

Final analysis: A good way to be seen, but expect to give out some goodies, or people will avoid your table.

Do a Fundraiser with a Local School

When my kids were young, we would get flyers from the PTA about going to a local restaurant on a certain night, and 10 percent of the proceeds would go to the school. I contacted local school PTAs with a similar offer. If anyone did Wash & Fold or Pickup & Delivery and used their school's code, the school would get back 10 percent. This also wasn't a one-night fundraiser. Every time the code was used, the school would get money, so it was in their best interest to promote it more. From the laundromat's perspective, you can't lose. If no one uses the code, it costs you nothing. You spend a little time working with the PTA president and maybe come up with a flyer. If it works, the PTA is doing the heavy lifting of driving people into your store. You give back 10 percent, which goes to kids, and you help the community.

Final analysis: It can only work in your favor, and the PTA promotes you.

Discount Codes

People love discounts and feeling special. If you want to, you can price it so everyone can get a discount. For example, if you need to make $1.50 a pound for wash and fold, you can price it at $1.67 and generously offer the discount. Ten percent off for police, firefighters, active military or veterans, seniors, students, teachers, nurses, EMTs, or anyone else you'd like. To paraphrase Oprah, "You get a discount, and you get a discount, and you get a discount!"

Final analysis: It's easy to do and doesn't cost you anything as long as you price it correctly

Plastic vs. Cash

Almost all laundromats today still accept coins. I think coins will eventually disappear since most people pay by credit card now, but it will take at least another decade. It's like cars. At one time, cars had CD players—the best technology available—but if you go new-car shopping today, you won't find any cars with them. Now, they all have Bluetooth technology. As the older cars are eventually taken off the road, no one will be using CD players, but that's not going to happen overnight.

When I speak of plastic, I refer to credit and debit cards as well as store-specific cards that can be loaded with money. All forms of payment have their pros, cons, and costs associated with them.

As far as quarters, customers don't complain about using them because they've always been used, so they expect it. For the store operator, there are no fees when customers pay with quarters. On the downside, as vend prices go up (the amount the customer pays to use the machine), they must pump more quarters into the machine. If there is a large machine with a ten-dollar vend price, that's an entire roll of quarters. Most people would rather just swipe their debit card. For the owner, it takes time to empty every box and refill the coin machines. The more machines you have, the longer it takes. There's also the possibility of theft. Coins are still money. In 2023, thieves stole two million dimes from a truck that was taking them to a mint.

Plastic makes it easier for customers to pay, and the operator doesn't have to worry about dealing with coins. Depending on your credit card processor, the money will be directly deposited into your bank account in a day or two, minus the processing fees. It also makes it easier to verify your income if you ever get audited or want to sell your store.

The in-house card system is a little different from debit and credit cards and allows you to do more with your customers. More costs are associated with using a card system, but the advantages are greater, too. A card system allows you to capture your customer's information so that you can market to them because they have signed up for it. It also allows you to run promotions. For example, for every twenty dollars a customer loads on the card, you could give them twenty-two; after ten washes, the eleventh one is free. Many owners decide to use a combination of coins and plastic because if the internet goes down, the machines will still take quarters.

If you have machines that only accept quarters, there are products on the market that you can attach to your machines that will allow them to accept credit and debit cards. It would cost you for each machine that you add them to, plus whatever your credit card processor charges to accept the payments. The good thing is that these are not all or nothing for your store. You could get them on your biggest machines and have people still pay by quarters for the smaller ones.

How to Increase Revenue and Profits

There are only two ways to increase profits. Bring in more revenue or lower your expenses. If you can do both, then you're golden. Let's start with the most obvious one.

Add Services

No matter how many apartments are around your laundromat, there comes a point where there are only so many people who will come to your store to do their laundry. The growth and potential in the industry are in Wash & Fold and Pickup & Delivery. Even as our lives are supposed to become easier with all our modern conveniences, people find themselves more strapped for time than ever. Any person doing laundry is now a potential customer for these services, which expands your customer pool to everyone. Wash & Fold and Pickup & Delivery have their own sections, so I won't proceed with them now.

You can also add dry cleaning services. There are two ways to do it. You could incorporate that service in your building if you have the space. There's a laundromat by my house that also does in-house dry cleaning. My word of caution would be not to do it in-house unless you actually know what you're doing. It's easy to see other laundromats doing it and think that since you're already working with people's clothes, you can just add that as another revenue stream. But you need to realize first that it's a separate type of business with its own special needs. The lady who owns the laundry by my house used to own a dry cleaner. She actually knows that business. If you gave me a dry-cleaning store tomorrow, I'd have no idea what to do.

Another way to add dry cleaning service is to partner with a local dry cleaner. This way, you can be a "one-stop shop" for your customers without doing the dry cleaning yourself. Let's say someone wants their pants pressed. You can charge the customer $10 and bring the dry cleaning (or they pick it up) to the cleaners, where they charge you $6, and your profit is $4. The hope for you and the dry cleaner is that your customers bring in enough dry cleaning to make the arrangement worthwhile. The customer only has to make one stop instead of two. Of course, if you have Pickup & Delivery, you could also pick up their dry cleaning. The only thing you need to be careful about is that if they aren't happy with the dry cleaning, they will blame you since you're the one who took their money, so you must partner with a quality dry cleaner.

Commercial Accounts

Don't forget commercial accounts if you're offering Wash & Fold or Pickup & Delivery: gyms, spas, barbers, salons, restaurants, physical therapy centers, golf courses, country clubs, hotels, Airbnbs, vacation rentals, long-term care facilities, etc. Even if they have their own facilities to do laundry, sometimes it's cheaper and easier for them to let someone else do it. My sales pitch is that even if they do it in-house, it's not free. They're still paying for an employee to do laundry and for the detergents, fabric softeners, water, and electricity. For the small difference between what they would pay us and what they pay anyway, why not just let us do it? It's one less thing they have to worry about.

A great thing about commercial accounts is that they're steady, predictable businesses. For example, if you have a physical therapy client, they will have roughly the same amount of towels every week and won't leave you for two weeks in the summer to go on vacation. A great residential customer could still have something happen that causes them to not use your service anymore. They move. Get ill. Lose their job. A business could move or close down, but it's less likely. You could look at this physical therapy customer as a $2,600-a-year customer if they brought you fifty pounds of laundry at a dollar per pound for fifty-two weeks. Many laundromats could easily grow their revenue and profits if they added just a few customers like this.

Remember that most, but not all, of your commercial accounts will want you to pick up their laundry and invoice them. If you don't do Pickup & Delivery, you can do the math and see if it's worth picking it up yourself or having an employee drive over and get it. It might not be worth it if it's a barber shop with eight pounds. If it's a country club with 150 pounds, you might want to figure out a way to get there. If you already do Pickup & Delivery, you will just add it to that day's route.

Regarding invoicing, they might want you to bill them once a month and pay you by credit card or check. When dealing with a business, writing one check at the end of the month and recording it in their books is easier than having fifty-two payments to input. You might also have some businesses that will leave a credit card on file for you to charge when you're done. Not every business will necessarily need service once a week, so that arrangement works for them.

Raise Prices

No one likes to raise prices, but it's a reality that we all live with. The question is usually about when and how.

You can raise prices for three reasons: 1. Because it's necessary, 2. Because you've added value, and 3. Because your competition raises theirs.

First off, life is expensive. Whether or not you raise your prices doesn't stop them from going up around you. Water, gas, electricity, rent, supplies, wages, etc.—they all go up every year. If you have to raise prices to make a reasonable profit, that's what you must do as a business owner.

The second occasion is when you make a major improvement in the store. Let's say you replaced a row of old machines with brand new ones, or you did renovations like putting in a new floor and upgrading the bathrooms. It's easier for the customer to accept the price increase when they see the money returning to the business for their benefit.

The third time you might consider raising your process is when your competitors do it. Don't worry about being less expensive than your competition. Focus on giving more *value*. In the laundry industry, people aren't going to leave you if you raise the machine prices by fifty cents or raise the Wash & Fold price by a dime if you offer them a good experience. People expect prices to go up. If you focus on value, you won't have to focus on price. Anytime you compete on price alone, it's a race to the bottom.

The next question is how much do you raise the prices (and how do you notify your customers)? The first part of that question is how much do you need to raise them by, and how much will your customer allow? If you're a good operator, you have some price elasticity. You could lose customers if you get greedy and raise prices too much. Another thing to consider is whether you only accept quarters or if people can pay with either a laundry or debit card. If you are bound to quarter increments, you need to think harder about it. If you raise a $2.75 machine to $3, that's a 9 percent increase. Most people can live with that because it only takes quarters, so there is no other option. If you raise that same machine to $3.25, that's 18 percent. You'd notice if eggs, gas, milk, etc., went up by 18 percent. You'd probably still pay, but you wouldn't be happy. Each additional quarter is a significant percentage increase, so you have to know how much your customers are willing to absorb. You can be more precise if you take cards on your machine. You can program that machine to $2.86 if you only need a 4 percent increase.

The second concern is whether you notify the customers ahead of time or not. I've seen the answer split on this. My initial thought was not to tell the customer. When you go to get gas on Monday, they don't tell you it's going up tomorrow. You just pay what they charge when you get there. When we raised prices, I was talked into giving the customers notice, and I'm glad I did. Many people who use the self-serve part of a laundromat are on a budget; they know how much their laundry will be every week. We didn't want to shock anyone, so in mid-June, we told everyone how much each service would change and that the increase would go into effect on August 1st. We put up notices around the laundromat so they couldn't miss it. We thanked them for being customers, and we also told them about the upgrades we were going to do. To my surprise, no one said a word about it. I was expecting some pushback, but there was not a peep.

Upselling

There are two ways to increase revenues. Get more customers or sell more to the customers you already have. Anyone in business knows attracting new customers is more difficult and expensive than keeping the ones you have, so you want to get as much out of your current customers as possible. You do that by upselling products and services. Years back, when you went to McDonald's to get a burger, they would ask if you wanted fries with that. Now, you would just get a combo, but back then, that was a way to upsell. The customer came in for a hamburger and a drink. Let's say that was one dollar for both (the good old days). The cashier would ask if you wanted fries, too. The fries cost twenty cents. If 100 people were asked and half said yes, McDonald's would have an extra twenty dollars in sales. So instead of $100, it's $120. Doing that every day adds up to a lot of extra revenue for that location.

You can do the same at your store. You already have customers coming into your store to use the machines. Upsell or mention Wash & Fold and Pickup & Delivery to them. Don't assume they automatically know you have those services. I know you might have fifty nicely folded bags of clothes they can see from other customers, but sometimes it doesn't click that they could be one of those customers, too. Or they might assume it's too expensive even though they don't know the price.

An attendant can also upsell in the natural course of customer interactions. For example, if a customer comes up to the attendant and states that they're going to leave the clothes in the dryer after they're done because they must run to the bank before it closes, that would be a great time for the attendant to say, "No problem. For future reference, we do Wash & Fold. Drop it off and we'll do the rest, so you don't have to run around trying to get back to us. We also do Pickup & Delivery, so you don't even need to leave your house." They may not use the service, but at least now they know it's available. The attendant gave them a solution to their problem: a lack of time, at least where their laundry is concerned.

Another place to upsell is at the register. If a customer brings in a drop-off for Wash & Fold, the attendant can ask them if they would like us to use the "house" detergent or if they'd like a Tide pod for a dollar. Some customers will say yes just because Tide is a national brand they recognize. I went on Amazon and picked out the first bucket of Tide pods they had listed. There were eighty-one pods for $20.24, or a quarter apiece. If you have ten drop-offs a day, and three people say yes, that's $821 a year in profit right to the bottom line, and all you did was ask if they wanted a Tide pod instead of the no-name detergent the laundromat used. With this example, I didn't consider if you could get the pods on sale or if the customers needed more than one. If someone drops off seventy pounds of clothes, they'll need more than one pod. The thing that I love about this example is how easy it is. An attendant on their first day can do this, and it shows how making even small changes can move the needle.

Stay Open Longer

If you're open for longer hours, it gives people more of a chance to use your laundromat. It's an easy decision if your store is unattended because there's no payroll. If your store is attended, then you have to consider the extra expenses. The first thing to consider is if there is any demand for longer hours. My laundromat closes at 8 PM, and I've thought about extending the hours, if not all year, maybe just for the summer. I didn't find any demand for our location to be open earlier or close later. It could be because the laundromat has been there for twenty years, so people already know when the last wash is, but not everyone would know that. We never had to turn people away. If your store is attended and you're considering longer hours, you need to figure out if sales will be enough to cover the extra payroll. Even one extra hour a day is about $6,000 a year in extra payroll and taxes. If you feel you will do enough business to offset the wages and make a profit, then it could be an easy way to increase sales.

Add More or Newer Machines

The trend in the industry is to have a higher ratio of larger capacity washers than the smaller twenty-pound capacity machines. People love the larger machines because they can do more laundry at once. If you had to do laundry for a family of five, would you rather do one load in a larger machine or break it into three loads for smaller washers? It's less work for the customer to use the big one.

Another thing you will find is that people use more machine than they need. They have a hamper of clothes and throw it in an eight-dollar machine when the five-dollar washer would be fine. As the laundromat owner, that's three extra dollars in your pocket. Often, laundromats put their big machines up front because some people won't walk any further. They'll just use the first one they come to.

Adding newer machines can sometimes lead to more profits. Much of this would depend on your current equipment and your competitive area. New machines usually mean you can charge higher vend prices. They are also more efficient than older models, as they use less water and energy to clean the clothes. Adding new equipment is expensive, so you would have to weigh whether the higher vend price (with possibly lower water and utility bills) would justify the cost.

Promotions

Everyone loves a sale, and promotions are a way to bring business in the door. The great thing is that there are so many ways to offer them. You can use the old-fashioned coupon. When we did those two township days I mentioned before, we gave out coupons for five dollars off any size blanket or comforter. You can discount days or times. Let's say Tuesday is your slowest day. You could discount each machine to $1.50. If you're a laundry that is very busy at certain times—maybe weekends—this can draw some of the cost-conscious customers away from those busy times and free up space and machines for people paying full price. If you have a card system, you can give people two dollars extra for every twenty dollars they load on their card. Maybe if you're using the card system, you can give a free wash for every ten loads the customer does. It's up to you what, if any, promotions you use, but the great thing is you're only bound by your imagination.

The other part of staying profitable is watching your expenses. One of the first things you will see when you research laundromats is that you should switch your washing machines to high-efficiency ones. I understand that is because there are a lot of companies that sell new machines, but it's just not always realistic. If you have machines that still have a few years of life left in them, you won't spend six figures to switch them out just to lower your water bill. What you can do is clean and maintain your machines. Anytime you have a repair person come to the store, it will cost you a minimum of a few hundred dollars. Several trips a year, and that adds up. If you learn to do routine maintenance, that can save you money.

You can put up signs to educate your customers on when to use hot and cold water. For most washes, cold water is fine and costs you less than hot water. Many customers don't know, and they assume things like "hot water is automatically better" or that "more soap means cleaner clothes." Another thing you can do is put sensors on lights so they shut off or dim when no one is around, which lowers your electric use. They can easily be installed in your bathroom or back room.

Look at your marketing and advertising budgets and see if they are producing the results you want. With advertising especially, you can spend a lot of money quickly by putting an ad in the local paper or running ads online. If they aren't giving you a return on your investment, cut them.

You should invest in technology to help save some money. If you're going to scale your business, you need it. I've seen my staff make mistakes with the POS that have cost me money. I can only imagine how many errors there would be if we wrote everything down.

If you have staff, do you need them as many hours as you schedule them? This would apply mostly to bigger stores with more than one attendant working at a time. Is a second or third attendant always needed? Could you, the owner, work any of the hours? I'm not talking about you quitting your full-time job, but if you come every Thursday night to collect coins and do some small managerial things, could you work the last two hours as the attendant?

Shop around. You'll buy things like commercial laundry detergent in bulk from a laundromat supplier. The same with your Wash & Fold bags and a few other things. For items like Tide, stain removers, bleach, paper towels, etc., it's cheaper to go to Costco or your local supermarket and buy them on sale. Procter & Gamble has a website, www.PGGOODEVERYDAY.COM, with special product coupons. They also have an option to scan your coupon for P&G products, and you earn points toward gift cards. I've also received prepaid cards as rebates from the site. Some apps like IBOTTA give you cash back on certain purchases. Luckily, many of the items are things we use at laundromats. I decided to do a large supply run at Walmart. I went on the P&G website, got my coupons, and later submitted the receipt to go toward the gift cards. I also got back over $50 on the IBOTTA app. When you own a small business, little things can add up. In this case, they add up in our favor.

Wash & Fold

"The idea behind fast food is great—people want convenience."
—Kimbal Musk (Yes, Elon's brother)

"Keep It Simple, Stupid!"
—This variation of KISS was first used by the US Navy in 1960

For most of the life of the laundromat industry, the perception was that they were for people who lived in apartments or for homeowners when their washer or dryer broke. With Wash & Fold and Pickup & Delivery, that isn't the case anymore. This is also why the industry's biggest days are ahead of us and not behind us. With these services, anyone wearing clothes is a potential customer.

When we bought our laundromat, my oldest daughter asked why anyone would pay us to do their laundry for them. I explained to her that our actual services are *time savings and convenience*. What we technically do for the customer is wash and dry their clothes and fold and/or hang them. What they are buying is the time they don't have to spend on this chore that they either don't want to do or can't do themselves. It's the same reason a homeowner hires a landscaper to mow their lawn when they already own a lawnmower. Or why someone would order food through DoorDash when they own a car.

I added the KISS acronym because I've heard people say that adding Wash & Fold is like adding another business. I might get some pushback on this, but I don't understand that thought process. Many customers come into a laundromat, wash and dry their clothes, and then fold them at a table. When you start a Wash & Fold service, you're doing the same thing the customer does on their own, except you're going to charge them X amount per pound to do it.

I don't want you to be scared off because you've heard of a few laundries that run a third shift or have dedicated pick-up and delivery drivers. There aren't many at that level, and most have been doing it for quite a few years. Just to give you a point of reference for where my store is, there is always something to fold, but we don't need three shifts. Sometimes, I call for backup if we have a heavier workload than usual.

The good thing is that you can start the service using "baby steps." In reality, that's how you will have to start anyway because even if you decide to start tomorrow, it will take time to grow that part of the business.

You will need to be at least partially attended to start. If you're already fully attended or plan to be, running the program is a bit easier. I'm not going to discuss how to promote Wash & Fold because I have already spent an entire chapter on promoting your business, so this will just be the nuts and bolts of running it.

If you are not fully attended, you must set up specific times that people can drop off and pick up their Wash & Fold. This might limit you initially because some people will drop off or pick up before or after work or on weekends, so you have to figure out what is best for your clientele. If you are fully staffed, customers can come anytime, and even if the attendant isn't involved in Wash & Fold, they should be able to take in an order or ring up a customer who is picking up.

You'll need a place to store the laundry that has been processed and is ready for pickup. If you are partially attended, you'll also need a place to lock all the laundry up for when there is no attendant on duty. Depending on the size of your laundromat, this is easier for some than others. I like to set ours up on racks behind the register so customers can see how many other people use our service and so it's easy to access when the customers come in to pick up their clothes. When we have more than we can put behind the register, we stack it on some less frequently used washers. Do I like doing that? No, but because of the size of my store, I only have so much room. I've seen this done in other small laundries too.

The second space you need is somewhere to store what needs to be washed. When we bought our store, the former owner was keeping this laundry up by the front desk, and it looked like my son's room, with dirty laundry everywhere. We bought shelving to put in the back to store it. The customers want to see the nice, finished product, not the mess before it's processed. When customers bring in their clothes, they come in all different containers. You'll get laundry baskets, laundry bags, big black garbage bags, recycling shopping bags, pillowcases, etc.

You know how I feel about the importance of a POS system, but I understand that if you're starting at zero with Wash & Fold, you might want to test it out before investing in a system. If you're already doing some Wash & Fold and want to scale up, you will need to get a POS system if you don't already have one. Either way, you will need to collect some basic information from the customer, such as their name, phone number, and email. You can ask for their address, but they may or may not want to give that for a drop-off service. If you write this down, you will need a receivable pad with the original page and two copies. One for you, one for the customer, and one for the bag/hamper/basket they are dropping off. If they are dropping off several bags, you must make a copy for each bag. If you have a POS, just print out the number of tags you need.

It's extremely important to tag everything. Let's say a customer brings in two hampers. You want to tag both hampers with the customer's name, order number, how many bags/hampers they brought in, and washing or drying preferences, if any.

Here's how the process works. The customer's clothes will go in a staging area, usually in the back. When the attendant is ready to work on the clothes, they'll go back and find them. If you have room, I recommend putting customers' orders in their own container or bin; this way if some clothes fall out, you know whom they belong to. If someone brought their clothes in a pillowcase and a sock fell out, how would you know whose laundry it goes with?

Say the attendant is looking for Levon's clothes, and he has six bags. Each bag should be labeled, and each label should state there are six bags. You could easily miss one if you don't know how many bags you are looking for. Let's say one of Levon's bags was moved away from the other ones because an attendant was looking for something. The person doing Levon's order sees a pile of bags and his order is seventy-three pounds. They grab the five bags, not knowing there is a sixth one with another fifteen pounds in it. The best-case scenario is this causes you some extra work when you come across the sixth bag and realize it wasn't done. In the worst case, Levon picks up the order and realizes some of his clothes are missing and isn't happy about it. One way to catch this before it goes out the door is to reweigh the clothes before they are marked finished, and if the amounts are off, you can start looking for the missing clothes.

Now, the attendant will wash the clothes. First, they should check all the pockets and ensure nothing was left in them. Money, tissues, medicine, crayons, and anything else you can imagine. Depending on the clothes, they might treat them for stains first or separate them out based on colors or customer preferences. Once they are in the machines, each machine that has Levon's clothes should have a tag stating what order they are in. You could have more than one order washing or drying simultaneously, and you don't want to be guessing or trying to remember which ones went into which machines.

When the clothes go into the dryers, the same thing happens. Each dryer should have a tag on it. It's also important to tag any hamper the order came in. If the clothes come in a laundry bag, we wash the bag, too. You don't want to give them back clean clothes and a dirty bag. If they bring their laundry in a large black garbage bag, we reuse the bags in garbage cans (weird but true fact, I've never bought garbage bags for the store). If they come in a hamper, you want to tag it, too. You don't want another customer accidentally taking the hamper. Remember that not all orders are done by one person. Person A can start the washing or drying, then person B relieves them and finishes the order. Person B would have no idea whom the hampers belong to if they weren't tagged. It could belong to a customer. It could belong to a Wash & Fold order, but which one? Tag everything. It will make your life easier.

When the clothes are dry, you start folding them. Again, I go back to KISS. If you listened to some people, you'd think your attendants needed to go to a trade school to learn how to fold. Every person reading this right now has folded clothes. It's not hard, so don't make it hard. It's something that comes easier and quicker to some people than others, but everyone can do it. If you are a bit folding-challenged, you can get a folding board for fifteen dollars.

The most important things about folding are quality and consistency. Yes, we can all fold, but I take more care folding paying customer's clothes than my own. They are paying you a premium for this service, so they don't expect to see wrinkles when they wear their clothes. People are creatures of habit, and they like to know what to expect. Unless a customer requests something specifically, everyone doing the folding should fold the same way. This will take a little training because you want to ensure that anyone who touches a customer's clothes does it the same way. One good way to practice is on your own clothes. You don't want a customer hoping they get a certain employee to do their laundry because they like how they do it. When customers get their order, they shouldn't be able to tell who did it. All they want is to be able to open the bag and put their clothes away.

So that's it. You take their clothes in, weigh them, and give them a ticket. You wash and dry it based on what they request. Then, you fold or hang their clothes, based on what they want, bag them, and give them to the customer when they show up. It's very straightforward.

A question you might have is, "How much will this cost me?" The good news is, not much. You already have the hardest part: the infrastructure to do Wash & Fold. You own the laundromat. The labor part depends on you and if you're staffed already. For some owners, the laundromat is their job and they can do the Wash & Fold themselves. For others that are already partially or fully attended, they have staff that can do it. If your store is completely unattended, then labor is something you need to factor in, but you don't have to hire someone full-time right off the bat. You wouldn't have enough clothes for them to process at first anyway.

As far as equipment, you need a digital scale used for commerce. I still see what I call the old "produce" scales used, where you put the item on the scale, and the needle swings back and forth until it settles on a weight.

That's OK for bananas or when you just need to approximate the weight, but you can't use it for business in 2024.

Normally, laundries set aside washers and dryers that are used mainly for Wash & Fold. This could be different for each store based on the layout. One thing you want to ensure is that your Wash & Fold doesn't interfere with your self-service customers. It's your job to work around them and not vice versa.

For supplies, you can easily go online and find a company that sells to laundromats and order detergent and fabric softener by the drum. You just need one each to start; they will last you a while in the beginning. Depending on where you order from, with shipping costs and tax, you will pay a little over $100 each. If you want to start smaller, go to the grocery store or Costco and buy fabric softener and detergent there. It will cost you a little more for each customer, but it's the most convenient way to buy a small amount. You can buy everything else at local stores at the beginning, too. Stain remover, fabric sheets, bleach, Free & Clear, etc. You'd have to order anything specialized, but you can find the basics to get you started in the household aisle at the store.

You will need special bags to put the folded clothes in when they are finished for the customer, and they are easily ordered online. Buy one box of large bags and one of extra-large bags, and you'll be fine. You should pick up hangers, too, for shirts, pants, and kid's clothes. You don't have to get crazy with these, either. Just get enough to get you started.

Here are a few more points to consider. Start with a twenty-four-hour turnaround time. Even if you can finish it sooner, I'd still quote them twenty-four hours. In the beginning, you won't be that busy, but you don't want to get your early customers trained on a very short turnaround time because that's what they'll come to expect as you grow the service.

This is how normal drop-offs look in our store: Let's say it's Wednesday at 10 AM. Joey brings in a hamper with thirty pounds of clothes. We'll ask if tomorrow at noon is good for him. He says that's fine because he can't get it until after work. So, we put him in the POS for a Thursday noon pickup. Tracy comes in at 12:30 PM with a comforter, and we ask if 12:30 PM Thursday works. She says she needs it today if there is any possible way, because her child is sick, and it's their favorite blanket. We know a blanket is easy because folding only takes a minute or two, so we tell her she can have it after 5 PM. Reggie comes in at 1 PM with his bag, and we ask if 1 PM Thursday is good. He says, "whenever," he's not going to pick it up until Sunday. I'd put him in the system for 5 PM Friday. I want to get him on the schedule, but at the same time, I want to leave room for the person who says they really, really need it by 8 AM the next day because they don't have any work clothes left.

If a customer has no specific requests, we use "house" detergent and fabric softener. We buy these cleaners by the drum, specifically for use in laundromats. We generally wash most things in cold water. This is less expensive for us and better for the environment. You only need hot water for certain types of clothes or if you're trying to sanitize the wash. For most laundry, cold is fine. We don't separate out colors and whites. At one time, this was something your grandparents had to do, but the way clothes are made today and with the detergents used, there really is no need. There are a few exceptions to this: for example, if bleach is requested in an all-white load. If a piece of clothing is labeled not to be put in the dryer, we will hang that item and contact the customer. It might not be totally air-dried when they pick it up, and we don't want them to be surprised.

Processing Wash & Fold isn't like taking a number at the deli where the next number in sequence gets served. We work with the customer to create a time that works for them and a workload that works for us. It doesn't make sense to do Reggie's order on Thursday if there are more pressing orders to be done because even if you finish it, he told you he won't be in before Sunday to get it. Of course, if you have a small workload, you can do his order on Thursday and just have it waiting for him when he's ready to pick it up. We work very hard to get every order done early, but many people who say they absolutely need it for the next day don't actually show up until four days later.

You also need to set a price. Fortunately, you've already done your competitive analysis from the previous chapters, so you know which of your competitors does Wash & Fold and Pickup & Delivery and how much they charge. I would charge whatever the going rate is in your area. Don't worry about trying to undersell the competition. Wash & Fold is a luxury. People will pay what it's worth. If you want to offer a "sale" or "introductory" price to drum up excitement and get the ball rolling, I think that's OK. I would caution you to make sure people understand that this is a limited-time offer and what the price will be when the offer ends.

Make sure they realize that this is a premium service, and the low price is to whet their appetite. If you don't have as many customers doing Wash & Fold as you had hoped when the offer is over, I wouldn't extend it. I saw a store in my area have a large Wash & Fold banner sale for their grand opening and wound up keeping that price for eight more months. Once most people start using Wash & Fold services, they don't return to doing their own laundry unless it is a financial concern.

Next, you will set a minimum weight for the order. Ten pounds is a good minimum. Our average order is between twenty and twenty-five pounds. It's really not hard to come up with ten pounds of clothes, but sometimes people don't, and they still have to pay the minimum. Let's say you charge $1.50 per pound with a ten-pound minimum. That means your minimum order is fifteen dollars for Wash & Fold. If someone has 7.91 pounds, that would be $11.87. They then get charged a minimum order fee of $3.13 to bring the order to fifteen. Occasionally, a customer doesn't like that, but we explain to them that it still costs us the same to run a washer and dryer with eight pounds as it does ten pounds, and there's also labor involved. I've waived it on rare occasions, but I've never understood why people in that situation don't just bring a little more laundry. If you're paying for ten pounds, that would be a good time to wash sheets and pillowcases. Those minimum order fees can also add up for a store. In my first year in our store, we made over $1200 off those fees, and for much larger stores, it could be several thousand dollars.

The last thing I suggest is to bring a small load to your competitors for Wash & Fold. See their process. Look at it from both the customer's and the store's perspectives. How long is their turnaround time? How well are your clothes folded, and what does the presentation look like when you pick it up? If you think, "Wow. They did a nice job with the folding," you know the minimum level your customers expect to see.

There is a lot of physical work involved with Wash & Fold but running it doesn't have to be difficult. The two things to remember are consistency in folding and having clothes ready to be picked up before or when you tell the customer they will be ready.

Pickup & Delivery

"The vision is that people should have the ultimate in convenience. Being able to get the things they care about on the appropriate device."
—Bill Gates

Now that you've conquered Wash & Fold, it's time for Wash & Fold on wheels. Thanks to companies like DoorDash, Grubhub, Instacart, Uber Eats, Blue Apron, etc., customers are used to getting what they want delivered to them. From the comfort of their couch, customers can order their dinner, groceries, prepared meals, prescriptions from the pharmacy, and just about anything else they desire. This is a great opportunity for the laundromat industry to piggyback on the groundwork that these companies have laid.

The good thing about delivery is that once again, you can start with "baby steps." I admit when I found out that the laundromat I was buying did Pickup & Delivery, I was extremely worried. I thought they must pick up in the morning and deliver in the evening five days a week. Since I worked full time, I figured if I could work every weekend at my job, I could fill seven of those ten routes, but I had no idea who would work the other three.

This is problematic for a couple reasons. The first is that I would be working seven days a week in this scenario, and that's not a sustainable pace. It would quickly lead to burnout and regret over buying the business. Secondly, I should have just asked the sellers. You might think that should have been an obvious question, and you're right. I wrote this book partly because my due diligence wasn't the strongest, and I want you to learn from that. As it turned out, they didn't deliver at night, so that eliminated half the driving routes right off the bat.

When I talk to people thinking about getting into laundromats and I tell them what a great opportunity Pickup & Delivery is, their first thought is that they will need a driver, truck, etc. I love the big-picture thinking, but I need to rein them in first. If they think they will start offering the service and immediately be busy enough to need a full-time driver and a truck, they're getting ahead of themselves. Just like with Wash & Fold, a few busy stores might require a third shift; these same few companies probably do enough business to require a driver or multiple drivers. They have been doing it for years and have built their businesses to that point over time.

So where do you start if you want to do Pickup & Delivery? I assume you're already doing a decent amount of Wash & Fold. A "decent" amount is hard to quantify, but it's where you feel you have enough business to make it profitable and worthwhile to add the delivery part. The second thing I assume is that you have a POS system at this point. If you have held out this long, it's time to get one.

First, you need to choose the times you're doing pickups and deliveries, and the distance you're willing to travel from the store. A POS system will allow you to choose what zip codes are in your territory, and if someone tries to put in a zip code outside that area, it won't allow them to place an order.

In the beginning, if you or an employee will be doing the driving, I suggest having a smaller travel radius around the store, two or three miles or fifteen minutes by car. It really depends on where your store is located. Three miles might take you too long if you're in New York City with midday traffic. Conversely, if the store is in a less populated area, three miles might not be a big enough area.

You need to consider that you have to multiply the time it takes to go to the customer from the store by four because you will be doing two round trips to that address. One round trip will be to pick up the laundry and bring it back to the store, and another one will be to drop it off to the customer and return to the store. So, if you have one pick up and it's twenty minutes from the store, that's forty minutes of drive time for one round trip. Assuming you pay fifteen dollars an hour, that would be ten dollars plus gas to pick up the order, and the same to return it. If you're going to do it yourself and not pay an employee, that's still taking forty minutes out of your day. The goal eventually is to have twenty or thirty other pickups and deliveries on that route, so you divide the cost of the delivery person between many orders and not just one or two.

This is why I suggest having a smaller delivery radius initially if you are doing the driving in-house. If you have a few customers within a mile or two of the store and you can literally be at their residence in four minutes, it makes your life easier and the service more profitable

There are also POS systems that allow you to integrate gig workers into your delivery route. Let's say you want to do Pickup & Delivery five days a week but don't have anyone to cover Fridays. You can now assign that order to an Uber driver (or to other services) and they can pick up the laundry at your store and deliver it to the customer, or vice versa. This is a great way to test service demand before investing in a truck and hiring an employee.

There are downsides to using an outside company for the pickups and deliveries. The first one is, will they show up? Odds are they will, but you never know. If you've ever had an Uber driver cancel on you, you know it's something that can happen. Secondly, you have no idea who might be interacting with your customer. It could be someone you would never have hired, but they're going to your customer's house to represent you. Thirdly, if the customer has a question or wants them to relay a message, there's no guarantee the store will get it. For example, the customer could give the driver their clothes and say they forgot to add a note to the order, but make sure the attendant uses Free & Clear detergent because her son has allergies. If the driver works for you, the store will get the message. With an outside driver, who knows?

There are several ways to calculate costs. You can charge a flat rate per pound, with a certain pound minimum. So, if your customers drop off their clothes, it can be, say, $1.50 per pound; if they choose to have you pick it up, it's $2.00 per pound. Most laundromats have a twenty- or thirty-dollar minimum charge for Pickup & Delivery. It's not worth your time to pick up five pounds of clothes. You might also see "free" delivery advertised, but as we all know, nothing is free. Sometimes, laundries do not charge for the pickup and delivery, but instead, X amount for fuel or X amount per mile, which is really just a service fee in disguise. If you do the service through a third party like Uber, you can have the customer pay the delivery fee. They are already accustomed to it from having used these third-party services in the past.

When you begin Pickup & Delivery, you must ensure that you can seamlessly integrate it into your Wash & Fold business. Most people choose next-day delivery. Not because they always need the clothes the next day but because it's usually the first option given. That means you might have less than twenty-four hours to clean and fold for the delivery customers while still taking care of your drop-off orders. This is why you always need to be on top of all the orders in the system.

Don't automatically assume who can or can't afford the service. Someone living in an expensive house would seem like a better candidate, but plenty of blue-collar workers, single people, seniors, etc., can afford it and may not like doing their laundry.

Everything Else

I tried to fit everything into the appropriate chapters, but here are a few miscellaneous topics you might have questions about:

Do Laundromats Close on Holidays?

It's your business; you can choose when to stay open or closed. I think most laundromats typically close on Thanksgiving and Christmas. Much of it will depend on your customer base and if you can find an employee who will work on holidays. For example, my laundromat closes early Christmas Eve and New Year's Eve, and we are closed on Thanksgiving and Christmas Day. Our first year, we stayed open on holidays, and either my wife or I worked. Since we didn't know what to expect, we figured we'd open up, and if the store was empty, we'd close early. To our surprise, we often did as well or even better on holidays. You might think, "Who's coming to the laundromat on the 4th of July?" but many people have that day off with no other plans, so they do their laundry. If you plan to have an attendant work a holiday, you should plan to give them some kind of bonus or holiday pay.

What Do You Do with All the Quarters?

Handling all the quarters was a big concern for my wife when we were looking to buy a laundromat. It's also a bit of a fascination with customers, especially when they see me emptying the coin box. The answer is rather mundane. I empty the coins in a large pail. Then I make the coin buckets the attendants use for Wash & Fold. We usually have seven buckets, and they hold forty dollars each. One pound of quarters is twenty dollars, so I weigh out two pounds of quarters for each bucket. I then dump the rest of the quarters back into the two change machine coin hoppers. If I have extra quarters, I take them to the bank, which has a change counter.

Should You Use Accounting Software?

Yes. The best one is QuickBooks. The good thing about laundromat finances is that they aren't complicated. For the average-sized laundromat, you need about three to four hours a month to do the books. If you don't have the time or don't want to learn the basics of doing your own books, then it's worth it to hire a bookkeeping service for a few hours a month. This will save you time and many headaches at tax time. As a business owner, you should know how your business is doing. If you need a business loan, the bank might even ask you to send them your QuickBooks ledgers, and they'll make their decision based on that.

Do People Leave Their Clothes Behind? What Do You Do with Them?

People usually leave small items that they drop or don't realize are still in the washer or dryer, like a sock or hand towel. We have a lost and found section, but most clothes never get claimed. Since we don't get that many lost clothes, we just use the socks as dust rags. We did have a nice comforter that a customer washed and dried. They left it in the dryer and never came back for it. After holding it in the back for two months, we donated it to Goodwill.

Where Do I Do My Laundry?

The answer might surprise you, but we do 90 percent of our personal laundry at home. I don't know what other laundromat owners do, but we will only bring an occasional jacket or blanket to the store.

Should You Replace Your Equipment with New or Refurbished Machines?

It depends on whom you ask. If you talk to an equipment distributor, they'll give you five reasons you should buy new, and they'll be right. If you talk with someone who refurbishes, they'll give you five reasons you should buy used, and they'd be right, too. It's a lot like buying a car. It depends on what you're going to use the car for. So, do you want a new Lexus or a certified pre-owned one?

The two biggest questions you need to ask yourself are about your budget and what you're using the machine for. If your budget is small, you can either buy fewer new machines or get refurbished ones. If you replace two machines you use strictly for Wash & Fold, you could probably save money with the refurbished one. If you've just bought the laundry, want to overhaul it, and plan to be a long-time owner, I'd go with new. If you want to sell the store in a few years, you might want to upgrade what you have but not put a lot of money into the store.

You can see that with these few questions, it really depends on your situation. If you do decide to buy refurbished equipment, make sure to go to a reputable company; there are many. They normally fix up the machines and give you a small warranty, just like if you had bought a certified pre-owned car. If you buy equipment from a laundromat going out of business, you're on your own.

Do I Really Need a Business Plan if I'm Not Getting a Loan?

Yes. Investopedia says ineffective business planning is the number three reason small businesses fail. How do you expect to be successful if you don't do financial planning, have a marketing plan, or do competitive analysis? Everything you need to write a business plan has been discussed in this book.

Do People Steal from Laundromats?

Unfortunately, people will steal from anywhere. Sometimes it's out of need, and sometimes it's greed. Even Winona Ryder got caught shoplifting, and we know she could have bought anything she wanted. This is another good reason to have cameras. It's also important to lock things up if possible or keep them out of reach. As I've mentioned, you want to be able to store your Wash & Fold somewhere safe so that a customer can't just walk away with another person's king-size comforter. If you're going to sell ancillary products that aren't in a vending machine, keep them behind the counter. As I learned in my time in retail, you can never stop stealing 100 percent of the time, but you can be proactive and prevent most of it. The number one weapon against theft is customer service. If someone wants to steal, their best friend is an uninterested employee.

Do You Recommend Any Other Resources to Learn about Laundromats?

I highly recommend that everyone join The Coin Laundry Association. They're the advocacy group for the industry, and throughout the year, they put on webinars and live events around the country to educate laundromat owners. They also have an online store to get information on almost every subject. If you're a member, most of the items in the store are free. You should also sign up for *Planet Laundry,* the industry magazine. It's also free, regardless of whether or not you're a CLA member. It will keep you up to date on industry trends.

What Is the Future of the Laundromat Industry?

"A bright future beckons. The onus is on us, through hard work, honesty and integrity, to reach for the stars."
—Nelson Mandela

Far from being a tired, old industry, laundromats are on the cusp of a new era. As our society looks for even more convenience in their daily lives, our industry will continue to grow and grow with Pickup & Delivery and Wash & Fold.

www.ingramcontent.com/pod-product-compliance
Lightning Source LLC
Chambersburg PA
CBHW070925290526
45795CB00001B/430